Ghost Stories & Graveyard Tales: Cincinnati

Allen Sircy

Table of Contents

Introduction

I never set out to write a book about Cincinnati, yet over two hundred pages later, here we are.

Initially, I was only researching eerie tales about grave robbers in the Midwest for another project, but I kept falling down multiple rabbit holes. When I finally came up for air, I realized I had amassed roughly fifty pages of notes. From opportunistic body snatchers to haunted burial grounds, there was too much material to not write a book about the Queen City.

While Cincinnati is known for being home to the first professional baseball team and its world-famous chili, quietly the City of Seven Hills has one of the most unique and complicated histories of any city in the United States.

After writing books about Nashville, St. Louis and Chicago, I thought I had seen everything. And then I started poking around in Cincinnati. From spooky tales to a doomsday cult, the stories are legendary. Oh, did I forget the historic music hall built on a pauper's burial ground?

Here it is, Ghost Stories & Graveyard Tales: Cincinnati! I hope you have as much fun reading it as I did writing it.

Resurrection Men

Body Snatching

Travel back in time with me to the 19th century, where graveyards were not peaceful resting places, but rather, a battleground for grave robbers and medical schools. In those dark and eerie nights, the moon cast an ominous glow on the tombstones, and the silence was only broken by the sounds of shovels digging into the soil. Yes, in that time, graverobbing was a lucrative business, and those daring enough to risk their lives were handsomely rewarded.

Across America, in cities like Cincinnati, medical schools were in dire need of cadavers to further the education of their students. The demand for these bodies was so great that some institutions had to resort to desperate measures, like employing grave robbers to procure them. But these fearless robbers weren't just ordinary criminals; they were experts in their craft, skilled in the art of digging up graves undetected and selling their macabre merchandise to medical schools.

With the rise of medical schools in America, the demand for fresh cadavers increased. The state of Ohio even passed a law allowing medical schools to take possession of unclaimed bodies from hospitals and jails, but it wasn't enough. The competition was fierce, and the stakes were high. For the schools, having enough bodies meant the difference between success and failure, and for the grave robbers, it meant the difference between life and death.

So, on those dark and eerie nights, the graveyards became a battleground, where the grave robbers fought against time and death itself to obtain the precious bodies. With every shovel of dirt, they risked being caught by the watchful eyes of the living. Yet, they persevered, driven by the promise of a hefty payday.

The shadowy world of body snatching was shrouded in secrecy, whispered about only in hushed tones among the daring few who dared to delve into its forbidden depths. The idea of stealing corpses was taboo, yet the profit margins were staggering - for those brave enough to take the risk.

Behind closed doors, professors and doctors turned a blind eye to the macabre trade, choosing to look the other way so long as their students had a steady supply of bodies to study. The dead were taken from the forgotten graves of paupers, discarded and abandoned by society.

But for those willing to engage in the grisly business of resurrection men, the rewards were great. The price for a single cadaver could fetch a small fortune ($800 in 2023), a veritable king's ransom in an era where many toiled for mere pennies.

Working in teams of two to four, they moved with the precision of a well-oiled machine. Each member had a specific role to play, and they carried out their tasks with a deadly efficiency that was both terrifying and awe-inspiring.

At the heart of their operation was the sexton, a trusted insider who kept graverobbers informed of new inventory. With his help, they knew exactly when and where to strike, waiting until the cover of darkness to make their move.

Once it was dark and people that lived nearby had gone to bed, the resurrectionists moved with lightning speed, their horse-drawn wagon

rumbling through the cemetery as they searched for a fresh grave. The air was thick with the smell of death as they dug down into the earth, their shovels and spades slicing through the soft dirt with ease.

And then, finally, they reached their prize: a casket, buried deep beneath the ground. With practiced ease, they opened the lid and tied a rope around the body within, hauling it to the surface with a desperate urgency that left their hearts pounding with adrenaline.

Occasionally, if the body belonged to a child or woman, the strongest member of the team would lift the cadaver up to the surface. Another member of the team would rush to assist and place the cadaver into a sack headfirst. Once the cargo was loaded, the goods were then loaded onto a horse-drawn wagon.

The body held immense value, but the casket itself was also a precious commodity. Determined grave robbers took great care to preserve the integrity of the coffin during their covert operations under the cover of darkness. A well-maintained coffin had the potential to fetch a substantial sum when sold or resold to local undertakers, ensuring a lucrative profit.

Old Man Dead

Of all those who chose to make a living out of being a
resurrection man in Cincinnati, the most notorious grave
robber was an Irish immigrant named William
Cunningham. Born in 1807, Cunningham immigrated to
Virginia before settling in Cincinnati as a young man.

Cunningham, renowned for his imposing presence as a
tall and robust man with a prominent jawline, further
enhanced his aura through his service in the Mexican-
American War during the 1840s. Upon his return to Ohio,
the burly veteran had a hard time finding work on the
docks. However, medical schools around Cincinnati were
paying decent money to anyone who would find and
bring them cadavers. Sensing an opportunity,
Cunningham assembled a team and started slipping in

and out of
potter's fields at
night.

Through the
years,
Cunningham's
choice of
occupation
earned him
notoriety around
town. In fact, the
hard-working
resurrection man had a handful of nicknames- Old
Cunny, Old Man Dead and The Ghoul were just a few of

the things that he was called. Though Old Cunny was a hulking figure, he was deceptively intelligent. He was quick on his feet whenever a member of law enforcement was around, and he forged long standing relationships with local sextons and grave diggers.

To get information about recent burials, Cunningham leaned on his friends that worked in the cemeteries. To show his gratitude, after big scores, Old Man Dead always cut them in on the profits.

In early February 1871, Cunningham and two of his associates, James Kendrick and Charley Johnson were flagged down by two police officers. Having been spotted riding away from Walnut Hills Cemetery in the middle of the night, The Ghoul was ordered to halt and allow a policeman to inspect his horse-drawn carriage.

As Cunningham jawed with one of the officers, Suddenly, the other officer's gaze landed on Kendrick and Johnson, who were seated on large canvas bags in the back of the vehicle. With a sense of foreboding, he demanded that both men step out of the car.

As they complied, the officer's heart raced with a mix of fear and adrenaline. What could be hidden inside those mysterious bags? With a trembling hand, he reached for the nearest one and slowly untied it.

What he found inside sent shivers down his spine. The bags were filled with human remains, a shocking and grisly discovery that left the officer reeling.

Old Cunny and his companions were promptly arrested and transported to the Ninth Street Police Station. As the officers conducted a thorough search, they stumbled upon a crumpled note in Old Cunny's pocket. Upon further inspection, it was revealed to be from a friendly grave digger, revealing the location of their latest haul.

Two men dead. Will be buried tomorrow. One died Sunday, the other Monday.
Yours, H. Gents
Please deliver this to Cunningham.

With the three resurrection men in custody, the bodies were sent to a local undertaker to be reburied. Before they could be taken back to Walnut Hills, two men claiming to be with the coroner's office came and took possession of the remains. They were never seen again.

Without the stolen bodies, the judge had no choice but to release Old Man Dead and his associates. Old Cunny was always a step ahead of the law.

On another occasion, after a score, Cunningham was leaving a cemetery when he was approached by a wagon carrying two policemen. The officers recognized the infamous body snatcher, but they weren't familiar with the dapper individual sitting next to him. Old Cunny called out, "How are you, boys?" as he turned to his friend and jabbed him in the ribs. The sly grave robber scolded his pal and said, "Brace up, Jimmy! The next time I take you to a wake, you'll get drunk again, will you?"

Realizing that Cunningham's friend had overindulged in a few beverages, the officers laughed and waved as they passed. But as the two horses went by, Old Man Dead's mare got a little jumpy. Cunningham grabbed the reins with both hands and his inebriated friend tumbled out of the wagon.

When the officers ran over to assist Cunningham's friend, they discovered it was all a ruse. The well-dressed drunk had actually been resurrected by the notorious grave robber. Once again, the wily body snatcher was hauled into the station and placed under arrest.

While Old Cunny was always watching out for the police, sometimes citizens would rise up and take the law into their own hands. One night after drinking in a saloon next to a cemetery, Cunningham and his crew headed out to claim two stiffs. Wise to his scheme, a group from the tavern followed the grave robbers and tried to apprehend them at gunpoint. After a brief firefight, Old Cunny decided discretion was the better part of valor. Although his associates managed to slip away into the woods, Cunningham realized he was outnumbered and agreed to go with the posse. Somehow, on the road to the police station, the crafty cadaver thief managed to talk the crew into stopping back by the saloon.

After getting each person drunk, Old Cunny promised he wouldn't steal any more bodies if they'd let him leave. In their altered state, the group unanimously voted to let Cunningham take his wagon and leave.

Naturally, the daring grave robber went right back to the burial ground where his men were waiting with the two cadavers. By the time the sun came up, the bodies were in the cellar of a nearby medical school awaiting dissection.

William Cunningham's zany antics were legendary in Cincinnati. But you didn't want to make him angry. After some medical students stiffed him on a payment, Old Cunny had the last laugh. Enraged by the slight, the conniving resurrection man exhumed the remains of someone who had recently died from smallpox. As you would expect, the young men were infected with the virus and Cunningham got his revenge.

On another occasion, Old Cunny hit the jackpot when he raided a cemetery in northwest Cincinnati where 38 smallpox patients had been buried. Cunningham dug each of them up and took them to the Ohio Medical College. Unfortunately for the opportunistic resurrectionist, the professors refused to take them, and Old Cunny had to return them to the graveyard the next night. When the sexton woke up the following morning, he found a pile of naked bodies in the burying ground. Before passing away on November 2, 1871, Old Man Dead sold his remains to the Ohio Medical College for $50. But William Cunningham wasn't just dissected and discarded. Old Cunny's skeleton was put on display in the school's museum.

Over the years the infamous grave robber's remains were lost to time, but his influence loomed large over the next generation of resurrectionists in the area.

Charley Keaton

One of William Cunningham's most trusted associates
was Charley Keaton. Learning the art of body snatching
from Old Cunny, the young African American made $3
per cadaver when he first started. As he gained more
experience, Old Man Dead increased his earnings to $8
for each stiff they collected. However, after a year or so,
Keaton asked for more money and threatened to go out
on his own. Not wanting to lose his colleague,
Cunningham made Keaton an equal partner in their
operation.

Unlike the Ghoul, who pulled bodies out of the coffin by a rope, Keaton often climbed down into the muddy grave and pulled the cadaver out with his hands. The burly resurrection man picked the stiff up and held it over his head before handing it off to Cunningham or another member of their crew. The remains were callously stripped of their clothing and dumped headfirst into a gaping ominous sack.

After collaborating closely with Old Cunny for four years, Keaton embarked on a solo journey following his mentor's demise in 1871. However, he wasn't left without support. In fact, his wife actively participated, assisting her beloved husband in carefully packing the cadavers into bags and discreetly delivering them to nearby medical colleges.

In an interesting side note, Charley Keaton was married to a white woman. Unheard of in the 19th century, the interracial marriage was mentioned in local newspapers as it was considered to be quite scandalous.

Unlike his old boss, Keaton didn't like being called a body snatcher. He preferred the term *subject gatherer*. At the height of Keaton's operation, when he was bringing in forty cadavers a year, the subject gatherer was bringing in $23 a body. Yet, over the years once schools were allowed to claim paupers from jails and hospitals, the prices dipped to $15.

Due to the unsafe working conditions in the brutal winter months, Keaton had issues with his lungs that would ultimately cut his life short. Knowing the end was near, the subject gatherer cut a deal with the Ohio Medical College. After collecting $35, Charley Keaton wrote out a short statement explaining that after his death, his remains were to be turned over to the school. On August 2nd, 1878, Keaton died from a pulmonary hemorrhage at the age of 40. After a small service in his home on Barr Street, his wife dropped her husband's cold and lifeless body off at the school just as he instructed.

Like other stories about Resurrection Men, there is more to the story.

Years after his death, Keaton's widow remarried. Oddly, the new husband died at an early age as well. When authorities dug into the untimely passing, it was discovered that the former Mrs. Keaton had been married on three occasions. Each time, her husband died an early death.

Although she was never charged, it was rumored that the "black widow" had killed Charley shortly after he received the payment for his remains and later murdered her third husband to collect on a large insurance policy.

The Ballad of Dr. Morton Part 1

Late in the evening on January 15, 1878, a startling discovery was made in Forest Cemetery in Toledo, Ohio. As the son of the superintendent was walking through the burying ground, he noticed a big pile of dirt next to the gravesite of 83-year-old Mary Leiner. But that wasn't the worst of it - upon closer inspection, he saw that her coffin had been forced open and the poor woman was nowhere to be found!

Police were notified and coppers started combing the area looking for suspicious characters. While security was beefed up around the cemetery, the next night, the final resting place of 12-year-old Charles Rall was found disturbed. And just like the recently interned Mary Leiner, Charles' remains were also missing!

On January 17th, a police officer spotted a man walking around Forest Cemetery. When approached, he acted suspiciously, and he was immediately taken into custody. At first, the enigmatic individual staunchly resisted cooperating with the authorities, providing them with scant information — merely disclosing his name as Henry Morton — and acknowledging his recent relocation to the vicinity with his family in late December. After being pressed about the disappearances of the two bodies, Henry admitted that along with his brother Charles, and brother-in-law, William Beverly, they had cut the old lady's body up and sent it Ann Arbor, Michigan in a barrel labeled *Pickles*. Before he completely stopped talking, he ominously warned the policemen "Better telegraph Ohio Medical College not to cut it."

Within a few hours William Beverly and Dr. Charles Morton, were arrested. A day or so later, the well-dressed doctor received not one, but two mysterious letters in jail. In a desperate bid to keep their contents secret, Dr. Morton immediately tried to burn the letters before officers could read them. Fortunately, he was subdued by two large officers and police seized the messages.

One of the communications was from an accomplice who specifically detailed what type of bodies the University of Michigan wanted and included a bank draft for $60. Afterwards, a search of the prisoner's house turned up shipping bills from United States Express that were dated the morning after each cadaver was acquired. Officers also found a large canvas sack, an auger, a shovel, rope and other tools commonly used by resurrection men.

After a few days in jail, Dr. Morton managed to obtain some croton oil that was smuggled into the jail. The wily doctor rubbed it all over his body and within days he was covered in sores. Five doctors were brought in to examine the prisoner and each determined that Dr. Morton had contracted smallpox. Once an emergency hearing took place, the Board of Health ordered Dr. Morton to the pest house. Though multiple doctors had made the same diagnosis, there was some suspicion that the physician was up to no good. Two guards were sent to the pest house with orders to watch the prisoner while he was isolated and receiving treatment for the dangerous virus.

After the sun went down on January 25th, a lynch mob formed in front of the small wooden building where Dr. Morton was being held. The group demanded that the grave robber come out and answer for his crimes. Dr. Morton cunningly called their bluff and told his guards that he would go ahead and turn himself over to them. Not knowing what to do with a man riddled with open sores, the group dispersed before Dr. Morton came outside.

Four nights later, with the shroud of darkness surrounding him like a cloak, Dr. Morton escaped the pesthouse while the guards were eating dinner. No one knows how he got away, but it was speculated that one of his guards knowingly left a door unlocked so he could flee.

With the doctor on the run, it came out that he didn't really have smallpox. Samples taken from his skin showed that his epidermis was irritated by the croton oil and that he was perfectly healthy.

Authorities searched high and low for Dr. Morton, but he was nowhere to be found. A few weeks later, the resurrection man would resurface, and he would make headlines all over the country.

The Harrison Horror

Only one man in American history has been the son and father of a United States President, John Scott Harrison. While his father was a hero in the War of 1812 and rode that wave all the way to the White House, Harrison took a different path. Initially he settled on a career practicing law but changed courses and chose life on Point Farm, the family estate in North Bend where he took care of his elderly mother.

Nevertheless, politics was in Harrison's blood, and he couldn't resist running for the First Ohio Congressional District in the United States House of Representatives in 1852. The son of the President served two terms in Congress before coming up short in his bid for a third term in 1856.

After the defeat, Harrison ignored pleas from various political parties to run for Governor. Instead, he retired from politics and returned to Point Farm where he remained until his death on May 25th, 1878. He was 73 years old.

Four days later, Harrison was laid to rest with his mother

and father in the family plot overlooking the Ohio River Valley in Congress Green Cemetery. Strangely, as loved ones walked to the burial site, they noticed something quite peculiar.

A week before Harrison's death, Augustus Devin, a relative by marriage, died from tuberculosis at the age of 23. He was also interned in the family burying ground near where the former Congressman was to be laid to rest. On the day Harrison was buried, Benjamin Harrison, his son (and future President) came to the gravesite and observed that Devin's grave had been disturbed. Initially, it was believed that a wild animal may have been rooting around in the dirt, but upon further review, they shockingly discovered that the young man's body was missing!

To combat potential resurrection men, John Scott Harrison's metal lined casket was buried ten feet deep in the ground as opposed to the traditional six or eight. The shaft was lined with brick and a stone that was so heavy, it took sixteen men to lift it and lower it into the hole. To further combat grave robbers, the family filled the grave with dirt and stones. At roughly twelve inches below the surface, the family also added a thick layer of cement.

Before filling the rest in with dirt, small wooden pegs were placed at surface level so it would be easy to see if someone had attempted to dig up the body.

Not wanting to take any chances with their beloved's remains, the Harrison family spared no expense and hired a private watchman to patrol the cemetery for thirty days.

After burying his father, Benjamin Harrison had to return to Indiana to resume his law practice and prepare for a speech that he was scheduled to deliver. In his absence, he asked his brother John Scott Harrison Jr. and cousin, George Eaton to go to Cincinnati to obtain search warrants for the medical schools in the area in hopes of finding Augustus Devin's remains.

Benjamin Harrison

The Jumpy Janitor

Once the family had obtained the warrants, John and George went to Miami Medical College along with two officers and a private detective who just happened to be the former Cincinnati Chief of Police, Thomas E. Snelbaker. The school invited the men in and allowed them to look around and made their staff available for questioning. After a few hours of poking around, the group turned their attention to the Ohio Medical School that had been rumored to work with unsavory body snatchers to obtain cadavers.

Oddly, the night before, a fireman claimed to have seen a wagon stop behind the school. But unlike usual livery wagons that normally dropped off cadavers into the "death trap", the vehicle the fire fighter had seen was a very nice passenger carriage. Before it pulled away, the fireman noticed that inside the carriage were three men armed with muskets.

As the search party stepped into the Ohio Medical College, their hearts pounded with anticipation, wondering what secrets lay hidden within its walls. They were promptly greeted by a jumpy janitor, A. Q. Marshall, whose eyes darted around the room like a cornered animal.

Marshall warned the group that any search on the premises should be done in the presence of administrators, but still he let them in.

Despite Marshall's reservations, the search party pressed on, their curiosity and determination fueling their every step.

Even though it was getting dark, the group searched the entire school from the cellar to the attic. Inside the cellar, a chute was discovered that opened in an alley where the fireman had witnessed the mysterious buggy the evening before. After bodies were dropped off in the chute, the cadaver was tied to a rope that was attached to a windlass.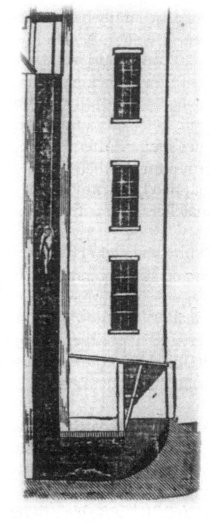

Someone on the fifth floor would operate a crank and pull the body up a shaft all the way up to them. Once the cadaver had reached the prep area, the remains were embalmed so they could be stored until they were dissected and studied.

The group walked the dimly lit halls desperately trying to find the remains of Augustus Devin. Every box and barrel was opened and searched as they went floor to floor. When they reached the dissecting room on the fifth floor, the men came across a student dissecting the head and torso of an African American cadaver. Though their stomachs were turning, the search party kept looking until one of the men found a large box filled with dozens of discarded arms and legs.

Thinking that they might find their family member's body hidden in the bottom of the box, the dismembered arms and legs were removed and set aside. Unfortunately, Devin's corpse was not in the box. What the group found was much more disturbing. Buried under the sawed-off limbs of pickled cadavers was the body of a dead six-month-old baby.

Taken aback by the horrific sight, the group pressed on. But by this time, they allowed the janitor to leave so he could notify school officials of the search. Yet, Colonel Snelbaker was leery of the skittish custodian from the start. Instead of going to find a member of the faculty, A. Q. Marshall ran off to a hidden area in the corner of the building. Realizing that something was off, all five men burst into the room where they  found a windlass and a rope that they believed ran all the way down to the cellar.

Wanting to know if anything or anyone was attached to the rope, Colonel Snelbaker walked over and tugged on it. Sure enough, it was taut and seemed to be attached to something heavy. Intrigued, Colonel Snelbaker slowly began to turn the crank. After a few tense moments, the remains of a man wearing only a tattered shirt with a cloth over his face started to gradually rise up through the shaft.

Immediately, John Scott Harrison Jr. realized that the body didn't belong to Augustus Devin. "He died of consumption and was more emaciated than this one," said John, as he started to walk away. Colonel Snelbaker wasn't so dismissive and advised him to take a closer look. "You had better look at the face," he recommended. "You might be mistaken, and you'll never forgive yourself if you allow any doubtful point to pass." John begrudgingly took the advice and stood there as the colonel pulled the corpse from the shaft and laid it on the floor. As Colonel Snelbaker pulled the cloth away from the corpse's face, John placed his lamp on the ground and leaned in to get a closer look. He was undoubtedly correct. The lifeless body lying before him belonged to an elderly gentleman, his countenance marred by severe bruising and an unsettling discoloration inflicted during the arduous trek from the burial site to the school. Yet, amidst this macabre scene, there lingered an eerie peculiarity — a man with an immaculate mane of snow-white hair, his beard abruptly severed at the chin.

Suddenly, John's heart started beating like a drum as he gasped and stumbled backwards. Colonel Snelbaker grabbed his friend by the arm and did his best to steady him. The room fell silent at the commotion. Staring at the cadaver in disbelief, John uttered the words that left everyone stunned: "It's father!"

Still grieving, John Harrison stood there stunned for a few minutes trying to gather himself and plan his next move. John sent a messenger to local undertaker, Estep & Myers to come retrieve the body and prepare it for reburial. John Scott Harrison's remains were taken to Spring Grove Cemetery and temporarily held in the P. B. Strader family vault where it was believed that it would be safe from other ambitious resurrection men.

Before John could get word to his brother in Indiana, the Harrison family in North Bend had already discovered John Scott's grave had been disturbed and his body was missing. George Eaton's brother Arch, along with John's younger brother, Carter boarded a train and came to Cincinnati to inform them what had happened. Yet, when they arrived, John told them that he already knew because he had seen his father's body at the school. Word was sent to Benjamin Harrison in Indiana, and he hopped on the first eastbound train he could find.

Scorched Earth

With the future President on his way to Cincinnati, the family members swore out a warrant for the arrest of A. Q. Marshall for receiving and concealing the body of the former Congressman. Marshall was promptly arrested, but within a few days, school administrators posted his bail.

When Benjamin Harrison finally arrived in the Queen City, he was ready to implement a scorched earth approach to dealing with the Ohio Medical College. Benjamin believed that the faculty hired someone to get his father's body and railed against them in the press. Not only did they not need cadavers since the school was not in session, but the lowly janitor didn't have a clue on how to embalm a dead body. Although someone at the college obviously had drained the blood from his father's body and started the embalming process, faculty members at the school played dumb.

"This must have been done by officials of the College themselves, and not by a janitor or subordinate, as they intimate," explained Benjamin Harrison to a reporter for the Cincinnati Enquirer. "Our family can accept no apologies or explanations from any member of the faculty who has any knowledge or suspicion of who is responsible for this outrageous act. We will accept nothing from them but a clear statement of the case. We do not want any hypocritical sympathy. We want information as to who are the guilty parties."

School officials played damage control in the newspaper and emphatically insisted that they didn't know who had stolen the body.

Typically, after dropping the corpse off in the middle of the night, the grave robbers went home to sleep and came back sometime the next day to get paid. With everyone in Cincinnati up in arms, the resurrection man who brought in the former Congressman decided to not come forth.

In defense of the Ohio Medical College, Dr. William Clendenin argued in the Cincinnati Enquirer that although all bodies were sacred, the work of grave robbers was necessary. Dr. Clendenin's counterpart at the school, Dr. Joseph Ransohoff went on record and claimed that the state should be responsible for providing cadavers to medical schools to prevent what happened to John Scott Harrison.

After verbally sparring in the press, Benjamin Harrison went on the offensive and requested another search warrant from Squire Vincent Schwab. With Augustus' brother at his side, Judge Schwab approved the second warrant.

On June 3rd, Benjamin and John Harrison along with Bernard Devin, Constable Sam Bloom, Inspector of Police Charles Wappenstein and several officers marched into the college to find the remains of Augustus Devin. Upon entering, Benjamin overheard a member of the faculty say that they were tired of having their premises invaded by "morbid curiosity seekers". However, once the warrant was presented, the staff member became much more helpful.

The search party immediately divided into two groups and began meticulously searching all five floors of the medical school. Although their efforts on the first four floors yielded no results, their luck changed when they reached the attic. It was there that Constable Bloom made a remarkable discovery. He uncovered a variety of items— a sock, an old coat, a woman's dress, and a shirt that once belonged to a soldier. As he moved about the space, his lantern illuminating the area, he stumbled upon more articles of clothing hidden between the beams of the roof. Upon closer examination, he realized that one of the garments was the very vest in which John Scott Harrison had been buried. Excitement filled the air as the men spread out, driven by their newfound momentum. Before long, they unearthed additional pieces of clothing, including red flannel undergarments, a black coat, and black pants, all of which had also been worn by the late congressman during his burial.

Benjamin Harrison took possession of the clothes and went back to the nearby Grand Hotel. When a reporter caught up with him that night, the future President told the writer that he was certain that the clothes were hidden by the college and that they placed his father in the chute to avoid detection. Benjamin let it be known that he was less concerned with finding the grave robbers, but wanted to make sure the school was held responsible.

After the discovery in the rafters of the Ohio Medical College, the administrators of the school were subpoenaed before a grand jury. Under oath, they testified that they had contracts with certain people around the country to provide them with cadavers for dissection and anatomical demonstration. According to the terms of the contract, the providers were not allowed to disturb private burying grounds or graves of anyone who had friends or family that would take offense to their body being taken.

The school subsequently announced that they were shocked and furthermore, if the men that they had hired were violating the terms of the deal, the school would not protect them. According to faculty, upon dropping off cadavers, the grave robbers were to place the remains in the dissecting room, shave the face, cut the hair and then inject embalming fluid into the veins. Under no circumstances were bodies to be tied up and left in the shaft. Moreover, on the night John Scott Harrison's body was brought in, there was no faculty present in the building.

While Benjamin was staying in Cincinnati, he was approached by a faculty member who claimed to know who the resurrection man was who robbed his father's grave in North Bend. However, when pressed, the man backpedaled and refused to cooperate due to fear of repercussions from Dr. William Wallace Seely, an administrator of the school.

After the discovery of his father's clothing and the discussion with the unnamed staff member, Benjamin

Harrison penned an open letter to the "Citizens of Cincinnati" to say thank you and try to sway them to his family's side in the court of public opinion.

"I did not suppose when called to your city by a message- the most shocking and horrible event sent to a son- that I should have occasion to address you except to thank you for your solicitous kindness and tender sympathy. That burden is heavy upon me this morning.

I can only say for the children of your friend, thank you, thank you. God keep your precious dead from the barbarous touch of the grave robber, and you from that taste of hell which comes with the discovery of a father's grave robbed and the body hanging by the neck like that of a dog, in the pit of a medical college.

But the purpose of this card is not to make any acknowledgements for kindness received, but rather to fix if I can, the responsibility for this outrage where it ought ultimately rest.

We have been offered through the press the sympathy of the distinguished men who constitute the faculty of the Ohio Medical College. I have no satisfactory evidence that any of them knew whose body they had, but I have the most convincing evidence that they are covering the guilty scoundrel. While they consent to occupy this position, their abhorrence is a pretense, and their sympathy is cant and hypocrisy.

Who can doubt that if the officers of that institution had desired to secure the arrest of the guilty party, it would have been accomplished before night on Thursday? The bodies brought there are purchased and paid for by an officer of the college. The body snatcher stands before him and takes from his hand the fee for his hellish work. He is not an occasional visitant. He is often there, and it is silly to say that he is an unknown. After being tumbled like dung into that chute by the thief, someone inside promptly elevates the body by a windlass to the dissecting room. Who did it, gentlemen of the faculty?

Your janitor denied that it laid upon your tables, but the clean incision into the carotid artery, the thread with which it was ligatured, the injected veins, prove him a liar. Who made that incision and injected that body, gentlemen of the faculty? The surgeons who examined his work say that he was no bungler. While he lay upon your table, the long white beard, which the hands of infant grandchildren had often stroked in love, was rudely shorn from his face. Have you so little care of your college that an unseen and an unknown man may do all this? Who took him from that table and hung him by the neck in the pit? Was it to hide it from friends or to pass his body in your pickling vaults for fall use? For a reliable informant states that an order has gone to gather bodies against your winter team. Your secretary has said, and I can prove it over his denial, that he thought he ought to name the man that did it. But he refuses my just demand that he should do so.

I denounce the man who thinks he knows the guilty party, and will not aid in my search, as the brother of that one who drew my father by the feet, through broken glass and dirt, from his honored grave. Have you advised him, gentleman of the faculty, that he ought to tell? Or did a change of purpose on this subject come from a conference with you? You profess to the public that you are extremely careful and solicitous that private graveyards shall not be violated. Do you expect to foster a careful spirit in your grave robber by covering them and making yourselves party to the crime when they violated your pretended instructions?

Would you not give the public better evidence of your sincerity if you repudiated the men who in their own wrong (if I was so), did this deed? I have not the composure to state my case clearly, but I think I have said enough.

If the faculty would have us believe them clear of a knowing participation in this crime, their conduct must be comfortable to reason.

The law and the common sense of mankind hold him who conceals the fruit of crime, or aids the escape of criminals, to partake of the original guilt.

Very truly yours, Benjamin Harrison

The Search Continues

After their adventure in Cincinnati, Benjamin Harrison returned to Indiana, while John Scott Harrison Jr. returned home to North Bend. However, the search for Augustus Devin's remains was far from over. The family remained committed to finding closure and pursued multiple avenues. They continued to pay Colonel Snelbaker for his services, but they also hired the renowned private security contractor, the Pinkerton Agency, to assist in locating Devin's body.

A valuable tip eventually led Colonel Snelbaker back to Miami Medical College, where he received information suggesting that a grave robber named Gabrielle had deposited Augustus Devin's remains and concealed them in the school's cellar.

When the colonel and a deputy arrived, they were greeted by a janitor who promised to cooperate and show them each room. As the custodian started up the staircase, Colonel Snelbaker insisted that they start in the cellar. Before turning around and walking downstairs, the janitor whispered something to his wife that caught the attention of the seasoned lawman. Colonel Snelbaker ordered his deputy to stay on the first floor and watch for anything that seemed strange.

As the colonel looked through every box and barrel in the cellar, the janitor's daughter caught the eye of the deputy as she tried to leave the building. When asked what she was doing, the child responded that she was taking a note to Dr. Clendenin to let him know that the hospital was being searched. After the deputy ordered her back to her room, her mother came out and tried to make awkward small talk with the officer.

Miami Medical College

When asked if her husband was going to be arrested, the deputy claimed that they were only at the school to locate the remains of Augustus Devin. Flustered, the lady grew more and more nervous before finally blurting out, "I wish we were out of this place, anyhow. My husband never did anything but what he was directed to do by the faculty, and if he gets into any trouble, they have a right to stand by him!" Once again, the deputy asserted that they were only there to find the body of Mr. Devin, and no one was going to be arrested. Relieved, the lady offered her condolences to the family of the young man and stated that she wouldn't want the remains of her loved ones dug up or dissected. At that point, Colonel Snelbaker and the janitor returned to the first floor. Aggravated that he didn't find anything, the colonel started barking at the custodian and let it be known that he wasn't going to leave until he had possession of Augustus Devin's body.

Once again, the janitor insisted that the remains they were looking for were not in the building. By this point the colonel could see that his new friend was starting to crack. Naturally, the old cop wasn't going to let him off the hook. Growing more impatient, he informed the frazzled janitor that he was going to have the cellar dug up and stormed off to meet with the deputy. A few minutes later Colonel Snelbaker returned and stood nose to nose with the janitor and demanded that he tell him what was going on. By this point, the school employee was convinced he was in trouble and was willing to make a deal to spare himself. The colonel promised that he wouldn't be arrested as long as he was helpful and told him everything that he knew about Augustus Devin's body.

The janitor's mind raced as he tried to think of what to say, desperately searching for anything that might spare him from the colonel's wrath. Although he stuttered and stammered, the janitor finally confessed that a grave robber named Gabrielle had received permission from Dr. Clendenin to bury cadavers in the cellar over the last several weeks. Though he believed the name was an alias, he was almost certain that the sketchy resurrection man was Dr. Charles Morton, a notable body snatcher that had recently made headlines for stealing bodies in Toledo.

Dr. Morton had been using the facility to store bodies before sending them off in pickle vats to a man named John Q. Quimby in Ann Arbor, Michigan. In fact, if the colonel dug out the cellar, he would find the remains of a woman that the body snatcher had recently hidden there. Colonel Snelbaker provided details about Augustus Devin to the rattled custodian, but he swore that no male cadavers were brought into the college around the time he had died. While the jailer didn't know for sure, he believed that Devin's remains were likely sent to the University of Michigan via the American Express Company.

Colonel Snelbaker sent for Dr. Clendenin, and within an hour, he arrived at the college. Unaware of what the janitor had told the colonel, Dr. Clendenin took both lawmen on a tour of the building. After Colonel Snelbaker and the deputy left, the janitor told his boss that he had come clean about Gabriel and the cadaver in the cellar. The administrator then instructed him to not do anything in the cellar until Colonel Snelbaker returned.

Under the impression that the janitor was lying, Colonel Snelbaker and the deputy returned later in the day with shovels. Unless he could see the body for himself, he was going to assume that Augustus Devin had been buried in the school's cellar. After digging in various places, the colonel found a large sack with a partially decomposed cadaver folded up inside. Trying his best not to vomit as he did his best to tolerate the awful smell of rotten flesh, Colonel Snelbaker finally verified that the remains were indeed that of an elderly woman.

After consulting with the Harrison family, Colonel Snelbaker met with representatives of the American Express Company and received a list of packages sent to Quimby & Co. in Ann Arbor. He believed that one of twenty large boxes shipped to Michigan on May 24th contained the body of Augustus Devin. The other nineteen likely held the remains of others that were stolen from a burying ground in Avondale.

Confident he was on the right path, the determined colonel made arrangements to head north to see what he could find in Ann Arbor.

As Colonel Snelbaker was starting to get to the bottom of things, Dr. Clendenin was scrambling to stay out of jail. According to an interview with the Enquirer, he had inspected the building after John Scott Harrison's remains were found at the Ohio Medical College but found nothing. Dr. Clendenin later learned that the janitor had been approached by Dr. Charles Morton, the notorious body snatcher. The devious doctor tricked the lowly staff member into believing that he was working with the school. Since Dr. Morton was on staff, naturally, he would be allowed to hide his stiffs in the cellar.

Before ending the conversation with the reporter, Dr. Cledenin further threw the janitor under the bus by implying that the custodian may have been receiving money from the resurrection man for his cooperation.

Michigan Pickling Vats

When Colonel Snelbaker arrived in Ann Arbor, he was surprised to find that there was no Quimby & Co. The company was a front set up as a front by the University of Michigan Medical School. All freight shipped to the company's address was sent directly to the institution.

With the help of the sheriff, the colonel coerced a janitor to let them into the school. Despite protests of an administrator, the pair made their way downstairs to the dark and musty cellar. To no one's surprise, they found three large barrels containing the remains of forty men, women and children. Much to the janitor's dismay, Colonel Snelbaker ordered him to pull the cadavers out of the pickling vats in hopes of finding Augustus Devin. As the custodian heaved the lifeless bodies from the murky pickling vats, the colonel's heart raced with anticipation. He scoured each cadaver, his eyes darting from one to the next, until finally, he saw it - a faint glimmer of hope that this was the young man he had been searching for.

Despite his eagerness, the colonel's stomach churned with unease at the thought of identifying a loved one in such a grisly state. He knew he needed someone who could provide a second opinion - someone who knew the Devin family intimately.

With a firm tone, the colonel commanded the janitor to leave the bodies untouched, knowing that even the slightest disturbance could ruin any chance of positively identifying the remains. He vowed to return in just a few short days, accompanied by a member of the Devin family who could help put his fears to rest.

After making a quick trip back to Cincinnati to meet with Bernard Devin and George Eaton, the colonel brought them back to Ann Arbor the following day.

As Bernard and George cautiously approached the lifeless bodies, their hearts were pounding with a mix of dread and hope. The air was thick with the stench of death, but they pushed through, determined to find their beloved relative's remains.

As they carefully examined each body, their eyes darted back and forth, trying to find any distinguishing marks or features that might help them make a positive identification. But despite their best efforts, they could not agree on which body belonged to their loved one.

Given that the bodies had dried out and their skin had an unnatural pinkish tint, the two argued over which stiff was Augustus Devin. Yet, after Bernard pointed out some scars on his body as well as a few missing teeth, George finally came around and agreed that he had positively identified the cadaver.

Epilogue

Augustus Devin's remains were taken back home to Ohio and he was reinterned in Congress Green Cemetery. After all the trouble the family went through, multiple people volunteered to guard the cemetery for the next month. Currently, Devin is resting peacefully in North Bend.

Today John Scott Harrison's remains are in the family vault built to honor his father. It is a short walk away from the family burying ground.

Regardless of the Harrison's feelings, no charges were ever brought against the Ohio Medical College or Miami Medical College for the theft of John Scott Harrison and Augustus Devin's remains. Civil suits were filed by the Harrison and Devin families but due to a fire at the Hamilton County

Courthouse, it's not known what the outcome of the lawsuit was.

Charles Morton, on the other hand, was indicted on two counts of grave robbing. Nevertheless, he never had to answer the charges because no one knew where he was.

Determined to bring Charles Morton to justice, Colonel Snelbaker went back to Michigan to find the dastardly resurrection man. Unfortunately, those at the University of Michigan claimed that they didn't know where Dr. Morton was or even how to reach him.

During the investigation, one professor confided in the colonel that if they were to turn the grave robber in, others in the dark profession might not be inclined to work with them. Ratting out a body snatcher would ruin the school and they would not have enough cadavers for their students.

The Ballad of Dr. Morton Part 2

So, what exactly became of our old friend, Dr. Charles Morton? Well, this is where it gets complicated and really interesting. After all the twists and turns of the Harrison Horror there is one more big one.

Dr. Morton had many aliases, Dr. Christian, Dr. Gordon, and Dr. Howard were a few of the names the slippery body snatcher used in the United States. His real name was Thomas Miller Beach.

Born in 1841 in Colchester, England, Beach embarked on a remarkable journey that would shape his destiny. While initially pursuing a career in medicine, his insatiable thirst for adventure propelled him across the Atlantic Ocean to the United States in 1861, a time fraught with tension and upheaval following the bombardment of Fort Sumter. It was during this tumultuous period that Beach forged his initial alter ego, assuming the name Henri LeCaron.

LeCaron enlisted in 8th Pennsylvania in the Union Army and served in the Army of the Cumberland under General William Rosecrans. Yet, as the war raged on, the young soldier grew tired of fighting and was thrown into prison in Nashville. Eventually he was released and wound up attending medical school at the Detroit Medical College. This explains his ties to the University of Michigan forty miles away. From the 1860s to the 1880s, Thomas Beach bounced around the country stealing bodies and working as a British spy.

Yes, you read that correctly. The dastardly resurrection man who stole the body of the son of a United States president was indeed working for the British.

Adopting a false identity as a Frenchman with a vehement disdain for England, he skillfully cultivated friendships with influential Irish militants who were active members of the Fenian Brotherhood. The Fenians, notorious for launching raids in Canada, proved to be a persistent challenge to the authority of the Crown. Leveraging his father's connections, Beach effectively relayed valuable information to intelligence officials back in his homeland.

It's thought that Beach used his political ties to get out of sticky situations like the Harrison Horror, as he seemed to just vanish into thin air when all the heat was on him. Beach likely went back home to England and laid low until things died down.

After settling back down in England, Thomas Beach released a memoir called, *Twenty-five Years in the Secret Service*. As you would expect, he doesn't mention anything about stealing the body of John Scott Harrison.

Thomas Beach died of peritonitis on April 1, 1894.

The Boy in the Haunted Tomb

On December 5th, 1911, several local boys were playing near the Harrison family tomb when one of them dared sixteen-year-old George Smedley to go inside. Eager to show his buddies that he wasn't afraid to go into the allegedly haunted tomb, the brave teenager opened the door and walked inside. As soon as he entered the crypt, he heard his pal's laughter followed by the unsettling sound of the door slamming shut.

As George lunged towards the door, his heart pounded so hard that he thought it might burst. The adrenaline surged through his veins, giving him a rush of energy as he desperately tried to turn the handle, but to no avail.

His mind raced as he frantically tried to come up with a plan. Should he try to break the door down? Or should he wait for someone to rescue him? But as the minutes turned into what felt like hours, George's hope began to fade. His throat was raw from screaming and his voice had become hoarse, yet he couldn't stop calling out for help.

The silence was deafening, and the darkness was consuming him. George felt like he was trapped in a nightmare that would never end. As he slumped against the door, tears streaming down his face, George realized that he might be stuck in this tomb forever.

A handful of people walking down the road heard the muffled desperate cry for help. Reluctant to investigate the creepy tomb, they assumed it was a rowdy wraith in the spooky tomb and took off running in the other direction!

Due to the crypt being partially underground, young George couldn't sit down due to water that had leaked in. After a few hours he almost gave up and climbed into one of the vaults to sleep but decided to yell for help one more time. Fortunately for him, Della Gabriel, a woman that lived in the area heard the noise. She courageously followed it all the way from the road, through the graveyard and into the Harrison tomb.

After four hours of being trapped inside, Mrs. Gabriel pulled the sticks that were wedged inside the handle and

opened the heavy door that had trapped George Smedley.

When George finally got home, his anxious mother scolded him and threatened to beat him before breaking down and smothering him with kisses.

The next day his story appeared in the Enquirer. Naturally, the reporter pressed him on whether there was a ghost in the tomb with him. George laughed and replied defiantly, "Shucks, there aren't any ghosts. Ghosts are to scare little girls with and people who don't know any better!"

The Tanyard Horror

After a string of fires ripped through Cincinnati in October 1874, a sense of dread hung heavy in the air. Still reeling from the sequence of conflagrations, the understaffed and underequipped Cincinnati Fire Department was summoned to the corner of Poplar Street and Gamble Alley on the night of November 6th.

When the local fire company arrived on the scene with their horse drawn fire engine, they found the three story Werk & Co. candle factory in flames. As the brave fire fighters struggled to contain the raging fire, the blaze spread to the basement where the boiler room was located. Without warning, a tremendous explosion ripped through the building and two walls came tumbling down. Amidst the chaos and relentless roar of the blazing inferno, three firemen were knocked off a nearby shed and fell to the ground.

As the fiery glow consumed the night sky, thousands of people descended upon West End to watch the firefighters battle the blaze. To get a better view, people climbed trees and made their way to the rooftops of surrounding buildings.

When the sun came up the next morning, fortunately, no lives were lost. Three firemen were scraped up pretty badly, but the worst injury of the night happened to Charles Barbes. Charles, an ordinary local man, found himself caught in the electrifying frenzy that gripped the air. Drawn irresistibly to the spectacle, he ascended to the pinnacle of Henry Freiberg's towering tannery, perched precariously above the bustling street. From this vantage point, he beheld the blaze that consumed a nearby building, its fiery tendrils licking hungrily at the night sky. Mesmerized by the spectacle, Charles leaned too far over the edge and suddenly felt himself plummeting towards the ground. Panic set in as he tumbled through the air, the wind rushing past his face as he hurtled towards the hard, unforgiving earth below.

The impact was brutal and sudden, sending shockwaves of pain coursing through Charles' body. He writhed in agony on the ground, unable to move, as a throng of concerned onlookers rushed to his aid. Their frantic efforts to carry him to safety were the only thing keeping him from succumbing to his injuries. When the doctor arrived, he informed Charles that he had broken both of his legs.

Charles Barbes' accident at the tannery was unfortunate, but twenty-four hours later, Henry Freiberg's building would become the scene of the most gruesome murders in the history of the Queen City.

Henry Freiberg's Tannery

Forbidden Love

In 1868, a seventeen-year-old German immigrant named Herman Schilling arrived in Cincinnati. Looking for work, the baby-faced teenager wandered over to Henry Freinberg's tannery on the corner of Livingston Street and Gamble Alley. Eager to help the young man, Henry hired Herman and started teaching him the ins and outs of tanning hides. Herman flourished at the tannery and after a few years under Henry's wing, he became his right-hand man.

Like others who lived and worked in the neighborhood, Herman Schilling often dropped by Andreas Egner's saloon next door to the tannery from time to time. Similar to Herman, Andreas was from Germany. He also settled in the area and opened a cooper shop on Findlay Street. After establishing himself, Andreas expanded his operations and opened a saloon with a boardinghouse upstairs on Livingston Street. Not long afterwards, Herman rented a room from the family and became a tenant.

The saloon quickly gained popularity among workers from the candle factory and slaughterhouses, especially after Julia, Andreas' teenage daughter, took up bartending duties.

Julia, a teenage temptress with luscious curves and a mischievous smile, had taken up bartending at her father's establishment. Her presence alone was enough to ignite a fiery passion among the patrons. When she wasn't skillfully crafting cocktails behind the counter, she would charm the crowd, effortlessly captivating them with her wit and allure. The air itself seemed to crackle with electricity whenever she graced the room.

Among her many admirers was Herman Schilling, who couldn't resist the beautiful teenager. Likewise, Julia's vivacious personality captivated Herman. Unlike the regulars, Herman stood out with his tall, lean, and muscular frame, complemented by his striking dark features.

Herman found himself spellbound by Julia's beauty and vivacity, and she, in turn, was captivated by his strength and enigmatic nature. Their encounters became filled with stolen glances, fleeting touches, and whispered conversations, fueling the fervent tension that simmered beneath the surface.

In the dimly lit boardinghouse, a clandestine romance brewed between Herman Schilling and the captivating young bartender. Despite the daunting ten-year age difference that separated them, their desires knew no bounds. Like shadows in the night, they danced a dangerous tango of secrecy and passion.

Under the veil of darkness, Herman would venture into Julia's chamber, the sanctuary of their forbidden love. The creaking floorboards concealed their rendezvous from prying eyes, as they surrendered to their primal desires.

Yet, little did they know that lurking in the depths of the household, a storm was brewing. Julia's father, Andreas, a stern figure oblivious to the affair that unfolded under his very roof, would soon shatter their fragile sanctuary. Fate, with its cruel sense of timing, set the stage for a cataclysmic encounter.

In the hazy haze of an early July night in 1874, the secrets they thought were locked away found their way into the ears of Andreas. The air thickened with tension as the fiery wrath of a betrayed father ignited within him. With a thunderous crash, the door to Julia's chamber was flung open, exposing their intimacy to the unforgiving light.

Caught in a cruel twist of fate, Herman's heart raced like a wild stallion set loose. Time became his foe, stripping him of the luxury to dress himself in modesty. Adrenaline coursed through his veins as he leaped from the warmth of the bed, his naked body bared to the world.

Andreas, consumed by a potent mix of rage and anguish, pursued his daughter's illicit lover. The pounding of his footsteps echoed through the corridors, each reverberation a reminder of impending doom. With each passing moment, Herman's choices dwindled, leaving him with only one option for escape.

Driven by a desperate instinct, he cast his gaze upon the moonlit night sky, an accomplice cloaked in darkness. The second-story window beckoned, a portal to freedom and salvation. In a daring act of defiance, Herman leaped, defying the laws of gravity, surrendering himself to the abyss below.

Needless to say, Herman was kicked out of the boardinghouse and had to find a new place to live. Initially, he reached out to a coworker Cornelius Westenbrook, but due to his large family, he didn't have a spare bedroom. However, his wife agreed to feed Herman each night anytime he wanted to come by for dinner. Around this time Henry Freiberg was looking for a watchman for the tannery. The pair reached a deal and Herman was allowed to move into a shed in the tannery yard.

While Herman literally landed on his feet after losing his room at the Egner boardinghouse, Julia's story was a haunting symphony of anguish and tragedy, a tale that would forever be etched in the annals of sorrow.

Betrayal loomed heavy in Julia's world, casting a dark shadow over her fragile existence. Andreas, once a pillar of love and protection, mercilessly cast her aside, shattering the bond between father and daughter. The once warm and welcoming home morphed into a desolate wasteland of heartbreak, leaving Julia exposed to the cruel winds of abandonment.

Yet, her suffering extended far beyond mere rejection. Hidden beneath the veil of her pain was a secret that weighed heavily on her weary soul. A life, innocent and unseen, blossomed within her womb.

But fate, in its unrelenting cruelty, dealt a devastating blow. Her father's hands that should have cradled her with compassion turned into instruments of brutality. The merciless onslaught of violence ravaged her fragile body, leaving her broken, both physically and emotionally. The precious life she carried was extinguished, a tragic casualty of the merciless storm that raged around her.

Julia's frailty compelled her to seek refuge within the sterile walls of the hospital. Days turned into an agonizing eternity as she battled against the relentless tide of despair. With each passing moment, her vitality waned, and her spirit grew dimmer, like a flickering candle on the brink of surrender.

And then, on that fateful August 6th, Julia's weakened heart ceased its feeble dance, succumbing to the weight of her shattered dreams.

With an agonized cry, Andreas Egner's world shattered into a million pieces. But as he struggled to come to terms with his loss, a fierce rage began to build within him, threatening to consume him whole.

In that moment of madness, Andreas Egner was a force to be reckoned with. His grief had morphed into a relentless fury, and he was determined to exact justice for his daughter, no matter the cost.

Grabbing two sturdy staves from a nearby oak barrel, Andreas and his son, Fred, set off like avenging angels, their hearts pounding with adrenaline-fueled rage. Across Gamble Alley they strode, their eyes fixed on their target: Herman, the man they held responsible for Julia's untimely demise.

As they burst into the tannery yard, the air crackled with tension. Herman tried to make a run for it, but Andreas and Fred were too quick for him. Like savage beasts, they pounced on their prey, their staves raining down on him with a sickening thud.

Herman tried to fight back, but he was no match for the Egners' raw fury. Blood flew and bones cracked as they rained down blow after blow, lost in their own world of pain and anger.

It was only the intervention of the tannery workers that saved Herman's life. With a roar, they rushed in and pulled the Egners away, their faces twisted in horror at the scene before them. But for Andreas and Fred, it was too late. The damage had been done, and nothing could bring Julia back.

After the attack, the Egners were fined and promised to keep their distance from Herman.

A battered and beaten Herman Schilling stayed away from the saloon and focused on his job. Yet, as he went about his tasks at the tannery, Herman butted heads with a co-worker named George Rufer.

George was unreliable and had previously been released from his duties by Henry Freiberg. But when Henry found out George's wife was pregnant, he allowed him to come back. Nevertheless, Herman and George couldn't get along and once work started to taper off, Herman advised Henry that George should be let go. After his shift on November 7th, Henry paid George his $11 salary for the week and told him that his services were no longer required. Dejected, George took his money and went home. However, a few hours later, he found himself at Egner's saloon drowning his sorrows.

The tavern buzzed with the hum of conversation, its air heavy with the scent of stale ale and the presence of desperate souls seeking solace. George, a man burdened by the weight of his recent misfortune, slumped on a wooden stool, nursing his sorrows in solitude.

But fate had other plans for George that fateful night. Across the room, a mysterious figure caught his eye — Andreas Egner. Sensing George's despair, Andreas made his way through the sea of faces, his piercing gaze cutting through the smoke-filled air.

As their eyes met, a spark ignited, an unspoken connection forged in the crucible of shared hardship. George found himself inexplicably drawn to the vengeful proprietor, as if destiny had summoned them together for a purpose beyond their comprehension.

In a whirlwind of activity, Andreas orchestrated a plan that would set their path ablaze. Swiftly, an announcement reverberated through the tavern's smoke-laden air, a thunderclap of disruption. The saloon would shut its doors prematurely, its patrons unceremoniously expelled into the unforgiving night.

The seed of retribution had been sown, and its tendrils reached far beyond the confines of that humble tavern. A storm brewed on the horizon, and Herman Schilling had to play for his sins.

A Trail of Blood

At 7 o'clock the following morning, Cornelius Westenbrook and his teenage sons, Thomas and George came to the tannery to groom the horses. Noticing the gate was unlocked, Cornelius called out to Herman.

A few seconds later, he heard a voice call out to him, but it wasn't Herman's. It came from the upstairs window of a house next door. A teenager named John Hollerbach said, "I shouldn't wonder if Herman was killed last night!" Confused, Cornelius implored the young man to come outside and explain what he meant. John hastily threw on his clothes and met Cornelius and his sons in the tan yard.

The night before, as John was getting ready for bed, he heard the sounds of men scuffling in the tannery. Having been friendly with the new watchman, he called out from the window, "Herman, is that you?" John heard his pal gasp for air and then cried out, "Yes, John! John, John, come and help me, someone is killing me!"

With fear clawing him from his insides, John yelled from the window, "Murder, murder! Let that man alone or I will come out and shoot you!" As John peered through the window into the enveloping darkness of the desolate yard, a shiver crept up his spine. The moon, obscured by foreboding clouds, offered no solace, casting an eerie pallor upon the scene. Suddenly, a sinister gurgling noise sliced through the stillness, reverberating through the air like a haunting melody.

His heart pounding, John strained his ears to catch any further sound. Then, as if summoned by the macabre symphony, he detected the faint echo of footsteps, their deliberate cadence growing closer. Each step seemed to pierce the silence, like the ominous countdown to an unknown horror.

A pervasive unease settled in John's bones, a feeling that something malevolent lurked just beyond his field of vision. The weight of the moment hung heavy, as time seemed to slow to a torturous crawl. The seconds stretched into an agonizing eternity, amplifying his anxiety.

Suddenly, as if the world held its breath, the footsteps ceased. A deafening silence descended upon the surroundings; the stillness so oppressive it was almost suffocating.

Against his better judgement, the young man flew down the stairs and ran out of the house. He raced down the street looking for a policeman on patrol. Yet, after an hour, he couldn't find an officer, so he went back home. John Hollerbach tried to go to bed but he tossed and turned fearing that something bad had happened to Herman. The moment he heard someone stirring in the tan yard, John jumped out of bed, hoping to see his friend alive and well. Unfortunately, it was only the Westenbrooks looking for Herman.

After John told his awful story, Cornelius sent his son Thomas to find a policeman. Together, John Hollerbach and Cornelius and George Westenbrook started poking around in the tannery.

Hearts pounding, their eyes widened as they entered the dimly lit stable, their senses assaulted by an overwhelming stench that made their stomachs churn. What they discovered within those weathered walls was a scene straight out of a nightmare.

The flickering light revealed a horrifying image—a manure fork, normally an innocuous tool, now transformed into a weapon of unspeakable brutality. Its prongs were adorned with a macabre tapestry of crimson-stained hair and glistening droplets of blood, as if the very essence of terror had taken physical form. But what sent a shiver down their spines was the inexplicable presence of a lonely suspender buckle, wedged tightly on the fourth prong, mocking their attempts to comprehend the sinister tale this place silently whispered.

Their gaze shifted, and their breath hitched in their throats as they beheld a pike, its once-sharp tip now dulled by the grotesque act it had committed. The weapon, dripping with scarlet, seemed to bear witness to the savagery that had unfolded within these walls.

But it was the blood-soaked broom, lying discarded nearby, that revealed the haunting truth. Each bristle seemed to hold a drop of dread, painting a vivid portrait of violence. Its connection to the nightmarish scene was unmistakable, a twisted accomplice to the horrors that had unfolded.

As their eyes swept the room, their gaze was captured by a sinister trail — a crimson ribbon, marking the path of terror that led them on a chilling journey. The floor beneath their trembling feet seemed to tremble with the weight of the unspeakable secret it held, beckoning them forward into the depths of the unknown.

Their resolve hardened, fueled by a mixture of dread and determination. Step by cautious step, they followed the serpentine trail of blood, its vivid red hue intensifying with each passing moment. It snaked and twisted, leading them through corridors and hidden alcoves, each step heightening the feeling of impending doom.

Finally, their relentless pursuit brought them to the foreboding threshold of the tannery boiler room — a place where the air hung heavy with the scent of burnt flesh and revenge. With pounding hearts and nerves stretched taut, they pushed open the heavy door, unleashing a gust of stale air that carried with it the weight of countless whispered horrors.

The dim light barely penetrated the murky chamber, casting eerie shadows on the walls as they cautiously advanced. The trail of blood persisted, beckoning them deeper into the abyss.

Time seemed to blur as they traversed the length of the boiler room, their senses heightened to the point of overload. Every creak, every distant drip, sent their pulses racing, adrenaline coursing through their veins. The group stood frozen with fear as they approached the foreboding boiler room. But they knew they couldn't turn back now. Thomas Westenbrook had gone to get the authorities, but their hearts were pounding as they waited for him to return.

Suddenly, the door swung open, and the officers marched in with determination. The group followed closely behind, their eyes darting around the room, searching for any sign of what had happened. As they stepped further inside, the faint scent of smoke and singed flesh hit their nostrils, sending shivers down their spines.

The specks of blood on the ground led them straight to the furnace, its fiery blaze sending heat waves across the room. The officers hesitated for a moment, unsure of what they would find inside. But they knew they had to act fast.

With caution, they pulled on the hot door handle and peered inside. Their eyes widened as they saw a large object in the back of the furnace, but the flames were too intense to see clearly.

As they worked to put out the flames, the Westenbrook boys frantically fetched buckets of water. Finally, the fire subsided, and the group was able to see what was inside.

To their horror, they found the head and torso of a young man. The remains were so badly charred that even Herman's friends couldn't be sure who it was.

The Suspects

Everyone in West End knew the heartbreaking story about Julia Egner and her illicit romance with Henry Schilling. So naturally, the police immediately centered their investigation 'round her father and brother. Officers Birnbaum and Knoppe, who had found the body earlier in the morning, were sent to the Egner saloon to arrest Andreas and Fred. The air was thick with tension as the officers burst through the doors of the bar. The patrons froze in their seats, their whispers hushed and their eyes wide with surprise. But there, behind the bar, stood the elder Egner, cool as a cucumber, tending to his customers and chattering away about the latest town gossip.

Little did he know, the gossip that night would be about him and his family. As the officers approached, their eyes locked onto Andreas and Fred, who were seated at the far end of the bar, their faces pale and their eyes darting nervously around the room.

The officers wasted no time in taking the two men into custody. Both were taken promptly to the Oliver Street police station and booked on suspicion of murder.

After detectives talked with Henry Freiberg, the owner of the tannery, George Rufer became a person of interest, and an officer was sent to bring him in for questioning.

Yet, George had already raised suspicions of two patrolmen who noticed him walking down Logan Street with blood and scratches all over face. He was also brought to the same police station and questioned by officers.

During the interrogation, George Rufer denied knowing anything about Herman Schilling's death. Despite his lack of knowledge about the murder, George did mention that he had overheard Andreas Egner say that he wanted to "run a pitchfork through him."

When asked about the scratches on his face, sweat dripped down Geroge's face as he talked about a terrible fall. But when he got to the station, he changed his answer. On second thought, George realized that he had been in an argument with his wife, Fredericka. Things got heated and Fredericka got angry and raked her fingernails down his face.

Alarmed by his inability to keep his story straight, the officers ordered George to be strip searched. George protested but eventually did as he was told. As he nervously slid off his pants and took off his shirt, a silence fell over the room. All the former tannery employee's underclothing was covered in blood. George stuttered and stammered and tried to explain that the blood came from a chicken that he had killed the night before. It didn't matter. George Rufer was now a suspect and placed under arrest on suspicion of murder.

Coroner's Inquest

The morning after the arrest of the Egners and George Rufer, the city was abuzz with rumors about the gruesome scene that awaited the coroner's inquest. As the jurors gathered at the behest of Coroner Dr. P. F. Maley, they were ushered into a room where a haunting sight greeted them.

The air was thick with the acrid smell of burning flesh, and the room was filled with a sense of unease and foreboding. As the jurors looked on in horror, they beheld the charred remains of the victim pulled from the fiery furnace at the tannery.

What they saw was a sight that would haunt them for the rest of their days. The seared, crumbled human bones, still held together by melted flesh and muscle, were a grotesque sight to behold. The cracked skull lay empty, its boiled brain on full display for the jury to see.

The jurors were left speechless, stunned by the sheer horror of what they had witnessed. It was a scene that would be etched into their memories forever.

According to the Cincinnati Enquirer,
The eyes were cooked to bubbled crisps in the blackened sockets, and the bones of the nose were gone, leaving a hideous hole.

At one point the coroner picked up the skull and peeled away some of the flesh from the mouth. As he was pointing out how the teeth were clenched, Dr. Maley speculated that Herman Schilling was likely placed in the furnace alive. When he pulled at the jaw, one of the teeth came loose and crumbled like baking powder in his fingers.

After the morbid show and tell, witnesses were brought in to testify in front of the jury. Henry Freiberg was the first to give a deposition. The owner of the tannery testified that he wasn't aware of any kind of confrontation, but he believed that Herman and George Rufer were not fond each other. He also mentioned that on the day of the alleged murder, Herman told him that there was no work and suggested that George be sent home. Henry acknowledged that he didn't really need George anymore, so he let him go.

Fredericka Rufer, George's wife, was then brought in to testify. After giving conflicting statements in broken English to officers the day before, Fredericka backed up her husband. According to her, after he was released by Henry Freiberg, George came home and gave her his wages for the week. As the couple discussed how they should pay their bills, George told her that he needed two dollars for a hat. This didn't sit well with Fredericka since he had just been fired. Like George had stated, she claimed that in a fit of rage, she scratched his face. After the argument, George did go out and pay bills, but he came home and was in bed during the time the police believed Herman was murdered.

After she was excused, Fredericka walked over to Dr. Maley and explained that she spoke German and apologized for her bad English. Fredericka then dropped a bombshell that instantly doomed her husband. She whispered in the coroner's ear that she had been lying. She didn't really scratch her husband!

When Fred Egner took the stand, he was noticeably jumpy. He told the jury that he heard George Rufer come into his family's saloon around 8 p.m. As the night wore on, he overheard him talking about getting even with Herman. Once George left the saloon, Fred claimed that he watched him march straight up Gamble Alley, through the tan yard and into the stable. Around 10:15 Fred heard a distressed Herman Schilling cry out, "Murder!" and yelled for a watchman to help him.

Once the inquest wrapped up for the night, the coroner and several deputies went into Fred's cell to see if they could get the rattled teenager to break.

As the moonlight filtered through the barred windows, a sense of foreboding filled the air inside Fred's cramped cell. The weight of guilt pressed heavily upon him, suffocating his conscience. With every passing second, the tension escalated, and the stakes grew higher.

In the dimly lit room, the coroner's piercing gaze bore into Fred, his eyes gleaming with a mix of curiosity and suspicion. The deputies, positioned strategically around the young suspect, exuded an air of authority, ready to pounce on any sign of deception. It was a high-stakes game, and Fred knew that his fragile web of lies was about to crumble under the relentless scrutiny.

Silence enveloped the cell as the coroner's voice sliced through the darkness, a sinister whisper echoing in Fred's ears. His probing questions hung in the air, like ghosts taunting a lost soul. How could the teenager possibly have witnessed the macabre scene unfold from such a distance? The implication was clear: Fred's involvement in this twisted tale ran deeper than he had previously let on.

The weight of the moment pressed down on Fred's trembling form. Beads of perspiration dotted his forehead as he struggled to maintain composure. His heart raced, thudding against his ribcage like a drum heralding an impending doom. The walls seemed to close in on him, trapping him in a desperate struggle for redemption.

Realization dawned on Fred, like a bolt of lightning shattering the darkness. He could no longer hide behind his fabricated alibis and half-truths. The gravity of the situation weighed upon him, an avalanche of guilt threatening to bury him alive. The room spun, a

whirlwind of emotions swirling within him, as he stood on the precipice of a life-altering confession.

With a trembling voice and tear-filled eyes, Fred Egner finally broke. The words tumbled out, a torrent of admission and remorse. The truth spilled forth, raw and unfiltered, exposing his tangled involvement in the sinister events that had unfolded. No longer could he bear the burden of deceit; his conscience demanded truth, no matter the consequences.

As the confessions echoed through the cold, desolate cell, the once-calm night transformed into a maelstrom of chaos and revelation. The night was far from over, and the truth had only just begun to claw its way to the surface.

Confession

According to Fred Egnar, George Rufer came into the saloon around 8 o'clock. Since they had run out of beer, his father was serving wine to his patrons. As the night wore on, Andreas kept needling George about Herman Schilling costing him his job. After several glasses of wine, George finally snapped and said, "Let's kill the low Dutch tonight!" That's all Andreas needed to hear. He seconded the idea and volunteered the services of he and his son to help complete the mission.

At 9:30 p.m. Andreas closed his saloon and the trio quietly walked up Gamble Alley. Using a key that George had found after Herman dropped it, they opened the gate and went inside the tannery. To keep the ferocious watchdogs on the grounds quiet, Fred brought some food to keep them from barking. As soon as they calmed the dogs, all three men went inside the shed and hid in the shadows.

Roughly thirty minutes later, the trio heard the sounds of footsteps walking down the alley and into the tan yard. Upon entering the stable, Herman patted the horse and fed it. As he was tending to the animal, George Rufer snuck up behind and hit him as hard as he could with a pine stake on the back of his head. Before he knew what had hit him, George walloped Herman two more times on the head as he fell to the ground.

A rush of adrenaline overcame the tannery watchman, and he started fighting back. Herman grabbed the stake with his left hand and pushed his right hand into George's face to keep him away. With Herman gaining the upper hand, Andreas rammed a pitchfork into his left thigh and dropped him instantly. As blood spewed from Herman's leg, Andreas pulled the pitchfork out and stabbed him over and over in the abdomen while George Rufer battered him mercilessly over the head with the stake.

Andreas Egnar

Herman cried out for help and begged his ruthless attackers to stop. Sadly, no pity was shown by Andreas, who plunged the fork into Herman again and again until he stopped moving.

After Herman finally stopped moving, a chilling silence fell upon the dimly lit room. The three men stood there, their hearts pounding with a mix of fear and anticipation, their breaths shallow and rapid. The weight of their dark secret loomed over them, intensifying the air of trepidation.

A flickering light cast eerie shadows across their faces, as George, with beads of perspiration trickling down his forehead, broke the silence. His voice trembled as he suggested disposing of the body in the vats at the tannery. The idea seemed plausible, for a moment. But as George mustered the courage to move the lifeless remains, an unsettling realization dawned upon him. It was far too risky.

An unsettling grin curled on George's lips as he turned towards the furnace, its insatiable hunger roaring like a beast waiting to be fed. A sinister gleam flickered in his eyes as he declared, "I'll slam him into the furnace!"

However, their morbid plan hit a snag. Herman's lifeless form proved heavier than anticipated, and their collective strength was not enough to maneuver him through the narrow doorway. Desperation took hold of George as he frantically sought a solution. In a desperate plea for assistance, he called upon the Egners.

Inch by agonizing inch, they managed to wedge Herman's lifeless shell into the doorway. But even in death, he seemed to resist their efforts, stubbornly refusing to surrender to the fiery abyss that awaited him.

A glimmer of hope flickered when Fred, a young and naive accomplice, tried to dislodge the stubborn corpse with an iron bar. With every ounce of his strength, he pushed against the inert body, desperation etched on his face. Yet, fate seemed to conspire against them.

Growing impatient, George snatched the iron bar from Fred's trembling hands, his eyes burning with a mix of fury and determination. With a primal roar, he summoned every ounce of strength he possessed and thrust the bar deep into the crevice, dislodging their enemy's remains with a bone-chilling thud.

The lifeless body tumbled downward; its descent halted only by the unforgiving embrace of the fiery inferno below. Flames lapped hungrily at the remains, devouring them with a voracious appetite, casting a macabre dance of shadows upon the walls.

A collective sigh of relief mingled with a sense of dread as the men realized the magnitude of their actions. The weight of guilt settled upon their souls, forever etching the memory of this harrowing night into their conscience.

With trembling hands and a lingering unease, the men fled the tannery, desperate to wash away the remnants of their sinister deed. Their footsteps echoed through the empty streets as they sought solace at a nearby hydrant, their minds haunted by the ghastly images that would forever haunt their dreams.

Although George was convinced that Herman was dead, Fred insisted that he wasn't sure and thought that he may have still been alive when they put him in the furnace. In all, Fred estimated that the group was only in the tannery for twenty minutes.

After learning that Fred Egner had spilled his guts, George Rufer told his version of the murder to detectives. While his story was similar to what Fred had told the coroner, George was an unwilling participant in Herman's murder. According to him, he had drunk a lot of wine so when Andreas suggested that they go over to the tannery to whip Herman, George was a willing participant. Yet, once the victim arrived and George realized that Andreas had taken things too far, he tried to leave the stable. But the elder Egner wasn't going to let him leave. He threatened to stab him with the pitchfork if he made a run for it. George Rufer put the blame clearly on the Egners and tried to portray himself as too inebriated to understand what was going on until it was too late.

The jury for the coroner's inquest unanimously determined that Andreas Egner and George Rufer were responsible for Herman Schilling's death. Fred Egner was also charged, but since he was a minor, he was only indicted as an accomplice.

As word spread around Cincinnati about the indictments, a lynch mob formed and came to the jail where the Egners and George Rufer were being held. Fortunately for the three suspects, extra officers were brought in for the night and the hostile group seeking justice was forced to disperse.

Court of Public Opinion

As all the drama played out in the local papers each day, the Cincinnati Enquirer started referring to the incident at Freiberg's tannery as *The Tanyard Horror*. Locals were glued to the newspaper each day to find out the latest developments in the over-the-top murder case that captivated the entire city.

With George Rufer behind bars, reporters started digging into his past. And what they found would definitely hurt him in the eyes of the jury when the trial began.

Leaving behind a wife and child in Germany to settle in America, George landed in Cincinnati but had problems with alcohol and got caught up with the wrong crowd. After being convicted of stealing a horse in the late 1860s, George spent three hard years in the state penitentiary. Upon his release, he came back to Cincinnati and met Fredericka, a housekeeper for a wealthy family in West End. Showing no regard for his family in Europe, George got married and had a daughter with his new wife. Sadly, George couldn't shake his demons and due to his struggles with addiction, he often beat Fredericka and had problems holding a job.

While it never was confirmed, it was rumored that George Rufer was involved in the fire at the candle factory the night before the murder. Apparently, Herman had seen him fleeing the scene just before the blaze and George wanted to get rid of a potential witness. Yet, since the fire was never mentioned in the inquest or subsequent trial, the story was believed to be only gossip.

Like George Rufer's alleged involvement in the candle factory fire, a juicy tidbit of news often dropped in the papers about either Herman Schilling or his suspected murderers. Others intertwined in the story like Julia Egner were also brought up from time to time. In fact, Julia's name was continuously dragged through the mud even though she had passed away a few months earlier.

It was speculated in the press that Herman wasn't the father of her child. A reporter quoted one of his friends saying that Herman openly talked about her having intercourse with multiple bar patrons. Due to her reputation, Julia was described in the paper as "a very loose young woman".

Even with her name being disparaged posthumously, public sentiment turned in favor of the Engers in the weeks leading up to the trial. Regardless of whether Herman had impregnated Julia, some believed that he should have married the troubled teenage girl and made an honest woman out of her.

On the other hand, a large percentage of Cincinnatians thought that Herman should've done more to make himself less of a target. With a distraught, heartbroken father next door, Herman should have moved out of the area instead of sleeping next door to the Egner's saloon.

Fred Egner's name also popped up in the newspaper as he awaited his day in court. Like his sister, the stories painted him in a bad light, but did help him in the court of public opinion.

It was speculated that the junior Egner was challenged and may have been autistic. He didn't know how to tell time and his family told reporters that his father wouldn't allow him to work in the saloon since he didn't know how to count. If anything, Andreas preyed on his son's naivety and inability to tell right from wrong to get him to help on the night of Henry Schilling's murder.

The district attorney decided to make a deal with the teenaged Egner, in return for his testimony and cooperation, Fred would only receive two years in jail.

The Trial

Going into the trial, the coroner, Dr. Maley, believed that Herman Schilling was attacked and put into the furnace while he was still alive. Yet, the district attorney thought it would be easier to get murder convictions for Andreas Egner and George Rufer if they claimed that the victim was dead before Herman was brought into the boiler room. Should the suspects renounce their confessions during the inquest, the defense could call into question the identity of the body that couldn't be identified.

Andreas and George were tried separately. When George's trial started on January 28, 1875, his lawyers, Willard Milligan and former United States Congressman and Senator, George Ellis Pugh immediately had their client retract his confession. According to George, he only admitted that he had a hand in the murder after he was given whiskey and assurances from the coroner that he would receive a lighter sentence.

On the night of the murder, George maintained that he was only an observer and was only there because Andreas gave him too much to drink. Nevertheless, prosecutor Clinton W. Gerard brought Dr. Edward S. Wayne on the stand to testify that the dried red substance on the defendant's underclothes on the night of the murder was human blood.

George Ellis Pugh

Despite the damning evidence, Senator Pugh argued that Herman Schilling was "a common laborer and his death is no particular loss." Due to his seduction of the young Egner girl, Herman basically got what was coming to him.

"It is told to us, not in wrath, but as the thing that will follow, that forever must follow those who give themselves up to that species of trampling on the rights of others that they will in some form meet the dreadful punishment which overcame this young man," exclaimed Senator Pugh. "It is the price of that sin, and all the laws made by man in all ages turn pale and fall before it, and one wrong of this kind forgotten does more harm than a dozen murders committed with a red hand!"

Due to the senator's conviction in the closing arguments, many in the courtroom were convinced that George Rufer was going to walk away a free man. Moreover, those present were actually placing bets on the outcome despite protests from the judge.

Twenty-two hours later, the jury returned with their verdict. George Rufer was found guilty of first-degree murder.

When it was Andreas Egner's turn to stand trial, he mortgaged his saloon and cooper shop to obtain the services of Major Charles H. Blackburn, the best defense attorney in Cincinnati. Like George Rufer, he was also found guilty.

Nevertheless, after both men were sentenced to hang on July 13, 1875, their high-priced attorneys managed to get the judgment of the Hamilton County Court reversed on a technicality. In the subsequent trials, Andreas was once again found guilty of first-degree murder and sentenced to death. Major Blackburn appealed the sentence and got it overturned to life in prison.

For George Rufer's second trial, Senator Pugh was granted a change of venue which meant a fresh set of jurors who hadn't been reading about the murder case every day in the newspaper. Even though a Butler County jury found George guilty, he was spared being hanged for a second-degree murder conviction. Like Andreas Egner, George Rufer was sentenced to life in jail.

Epilogue

After spending two years behind bars, Fred Egnar was released from jail. He went home and helped his mother, Margaret run the family saloon and boardinghouse.

Unfortunately, the news accounts of Fred's mental capacity were accurate. He nearly cut off one of his legs working in his father's cooper shop and developed blood poisoning. Fred Egnar died at the age of 34 on October 22, 1892.

As for his father, Andreas served twenty years in prison before contracting tuberculosis. Because of his bouts with consumption, the elder Egner started developing mental problems and was deemed insane by the courts. Since the prison doctors could do little for him, Andreas was pardoned by Governor Charles Foster and released from prison in 1895. Upon returning home, Andreas was subjected to bouts of mania and was convinced people were trying to kill him. The convicted murderer was so paranoid and despondent that he tried to drown himself on several occasions. In mid-January 1889, Andreas jumped in the canal during a brutal snowstorm. Though some neighbors managed to pull him out, he contracted bronchitis and never recovered. He passed away on January 23rd at the age of 57.

After Andreas Egner's death, his attorney, Major Blackburne, went on record stating that he felt that his client deserved to be punished for his part in the murder of Herman Schilling. Furthermore, he also believed that

George Rufer was drunk and only there because Andreas had served him multiple glasses of wine leading up to the Tanyard Horror.

And as for George, he had it just as rough as the old saloon owner. One year into his prison sentence, he lost his right hand in an accident while working in the facility. With the use of only one hand, George Rufer was a model prisoner and kept his nose clean behind bars. At the behest of Clinton W. Gerard, the prosecuting attorney in his case, Governor William McKinley pardoned George on November 29, 1894. After his release, he lived to be an old man and was said to have worked odd jobs in Cincinnati until his death at the turn of the 20th century.

George's wife, Fredericka didn't fare as well. Once her husband became a household name in town, she slowly went insane. After being arrested for throwing her young daughter Matilda against a trunk, the child was taken away and sent to an orphanage. A short time later, Frederick was deemed insane and sent to Longview Asylum.

Hauntings

Due to all the twists and turns and ups and downs in the tragic tale of Herman Schilling, it's only fitting to end it with not just one ghost story but two.

Fredericka Rufer didn't spend the rest of her life in the insane asylum. She actually lived a long life like her husband. But Fredericka carried her husband's sins with her for the rest of her days. In 1897 she was arrested for trying to burn down the boarding house on Plum Street where she had been staying. A night watchman found Fredericka trying to set fire to paper that had been saturated with lamp oil in the hallway. When she was questioned about her actions, the, watchman could hardly comprehend the chilling confession that spilled forth from Fredericka's quivering lips. Her voice, cracked and filled with anguish, revealing the torment that plagued her soul. She spoke of the relentless specter of Herman Schilling that followed her! According to her, the only way to purge herself of this miserable existence was to burn the entire building to the ground.

And as for that ghost that tormented Fredericka, according to legend, it also inhabited the tanyard. The townsfolk, consumed by a morbid curiosity, couldn't resist the lure of the supernatural. They spoke of the tormented spirit of Herman Schilling, forever trapped in a spectral form, his once-human flesh burnt to a crisp.

The Egner saloon became a gathering place for those who knew the tragic tale and wanted to find out if it was true.

Liquid courage flowed freely as they fortified themselves for the ordeal that awaited them. Bravado disguised fear, and one by one, they ventured down Gamble Alley, a path rumored to be cursed.

Like moths to a flame, they approached the forbidding fence that guarded the tan yard, the very site where Herman Schilling met his untimely demise. Trepidation clutched their hearts as they peered over, eyes wide with terror, hoping to catch a glimpse of the charred phantom. The brave few who dared to look beheld a sight that would haunt them until their dying days — a twisted, blackened figure, skeletal in form, haunting the tan yard under the moon's desolate glow.

Then came the fateful night when the cattleman from Kansas City arrived, his skepticism pulsating through his veins. Oblivious to the danger that awaited him, he entered Egner's saloon, unaware of the chilling tales that circulated within its walls. Intrigued by the local legend, he made a solemn vow to debunk the notion of ghosts once and for all.

Liquid courage swirled in his glass, emboldening him to embark on a perilous quest. With each sip, his skepticism grew, his resolve hardened. Finishing his beer, he emerged into the night, venturing down Gamble Alley, ignorant of the malevolent forces that lay in wait.

As he approached the dreaded fence, a creeping unease settled over him, like icy tendrils snaking around his body. With trembling hands, he mustered the courage to climb, his heart pounding in his chest. But as he reached the apex, a malevolent presence enveloped him, an otherworldly force that defied reason.

The air grew suffocating, thick with an otherworldly darkness that seeped into his very soul. Unseen eyes bore into his being, stripping away his skepticism with a merciless intensity. A bloodcurdling scream tore from his throat as he descended from the fence in a frenzied panic. Fear propelled him backwards, his legs carrying him in a desperate race for survival.

Dawn broke, casting a feeble light upon the town. The cattleman's absence raised concern among his friends, who sought aid from the indifferent police force. Their pleas fell on deaf ears, as the officers dismissed their fears with mocking laughter. Perhaps the rumors were true. Maybe the ghost of Herman Schilling had claimed the man from Kansas City, carrying him away into the clutches of the unknown.

No one knows for sure what happened to the cattleman, but a sarcastic police officer did tell reporters that he would go to Freiberg's tannery to try to see if Herman would confess.

Arsenic Anna

After conceiving a baby boy out of wedlock with a married man, Anna Marie Filcher was shunned by her family in Germany. Once the little Oscar was born, Anna left him with relatives and came to Cincinnati in 1929 to live with her uncle, Johannes Oswald. Sadly, not long after she got settled, Johannes died suddenly. Despite the tragic loss, Anna benefited greatly and was surprisingly named as the sole heir in his will. Though she had to start over again, at least she had $1,000 and some stock that her uncle had left her.

Shortly after the death of Uncle Johannes, Anna met a young German man named Phillip Hahn at a dance. Phillip fell hard for the portly single mother with blonde hair and blue-gray eyes and a whirlwind courtship ensued. Though they didn't really know each other very well, within a few weeks, the pair were married. Ernst Kohler, an elderly friend of Anna's father, invited the newlyweds to move in with him on Colerain Avenue. Finally having some stability, Anna went back overseas and brought her little boy, Oscar to Ohio.

A short time after Oscar got acclimated to his new home, Ernst's health took a turn, and the senior citizen became very ill. In his last days, Anna took care of him and nursed him until he drew his last breath. Once again, after the loss of a loved one, fortune smiled upon Anna. Ernst, the old family friend, left his residence on Colerain Avenue to Anna and Phillip. In honor of Ernst's generosity, Anna kept his ashes on display in a can on the mantle of the fireplace.

Things were looking up for Anna and Phillip, so they decided to start a business and opened a bakery. Unfortunately, the company never caught on during the Great Depression and the couple was forced to rent out rooms in their house to make ends meet.

After the business failed, Anna spent a lot of her time at the horse track betting on the ponies. Having spent up all her good luck on inheritances in recent years, she didn't fare well at the track. Even though her house was paid off, Anna took out a mortgage to try to win back what she had lost. Having already dug herself in a deep hole, Anna did what most degenerate gamblers do; she kept on digging. It took a month or two, but Anna burned through the rest of the money that the bank had loaned her at the track.

Deep in debt, Anna made a friend at the track. In 1935 she started palling around with Albert Palmer, an elderly retiree who also liked to hang around the track and indulge himself with alcohol. The old railroad man wasn't expecting the advances of the overweight housewife, but he also wasn't going to push her away. Anna paid numerous calls and wrote a handful of letters to her new friend. She painted a rosy picture of her finances and claimed to have valuable stocks but wasn't able to access them. However, due to the bakery failing, Anna had been having issues with creditors who wanted their money as soon as possible.

Palmer readily agreed to help the flirtatious young woman and loaned her $2,000 ($45,000 in 2023). Nevertheless, in early 1936 the naïve senior citizen started to realize that Anna probably didn't have the money to repay him. One night when she came by Palmer demanded that she pay back the loan immediately. Anna agreed but asked for a few weeks to get the funds together. Growing even more suspicious, Palmer reluctantly gave his much younger friend the benefit of the doubt.

Scrambling to come up with money to pay Albert back, Anna stopped by the residence of 62-year-old George Heis, who lived nearby. Heis was a successful coal dealer who was believed to be very wealthy. Trying to fill him out, Anna placed an order for coal and spent some time making friendly conversation with Heis. The next day Anna came back to see him, but regrettably, she didn't have the funds to pay for the coal, so she had to cancel the order. Nevertheless, Anna told her new friend that she knew some people who needed coal and she would put him into contact with them.

The following day, Anna stopped by again. Heis didn't mind. Like Palmer, the aging bachelor also enjoyed the dalliance with a younger woman. Once Anna batted her blue eyes and gave her song and dance about her failed business, the wealthy coal dealer gladly lent her $2,000.

It was a dark and stormy night on March 27, 1936, when Albert Palmer arrived at Anna's doorstep expecting his money. He had a deadline for her and wasn't going to let her forget it. As they sat together, tension hung thick in the air like a shroud, suffocating any hope for a peaceful resolution.

But things took a deadly turn when Palmer demanded that Anna prepare some oysters that he had brought with him. Little did he know that Anna had already hatched a devious plan. With her heart pounding like a jackhammer, she snuck down to the basement, her fingers trembling as she reached for the rat poison hidden behind a stack of boxes.

With the poison expertly mixed into the oysters, Anna watched as Palmer greedily consumed them, a sinister grin spreading across her face as she waited for the deadly effects to take hold. Within a few short hours, her creditor was gone, his once-threatening presence reduced to nothing more than a memory.

And yet, as the days passed, no one suspected a thing. Old people die all the time, after all.

With Albert Palmer vanquished, the menacing presence of George Heis loomed ominously over Anna. Each passing day brought his relentless inquiries about the money he had lent her, and the walls of her world closed in as the deadline approached. Desperation clawed at her heart, and she knew that time was slipping through her fingers like grains of sand in an hourglass.

One moonlit evening, a cloak of secrecy draped around Anna as she concocted a plan. Her hands trembled slightly as she carefully poured a glass of beer and approached George Heis, wearing a mask of innocence. Engaging him in idle conversation, she lured him deeper into her web, his senses dulled by the frothy amber elixir that danced upon his lips.

Unbeknownst to Heis, a sinister twist was lurking in the shadows. As Anna exited the room, a shiver ran down Heis' spine. A peculiar sight befell his gaze, as he witnessed the flies that had taken a fateful sip from the beer plummeting lifeless onto the table before him. The room grew colder, and a chilling sense of foreboding crept up his spine like icy tendrils.

Later that night, plagued by an inexplicable unease, Heis confessed to Anna that he was feeling unwell. Her eyes gleamed with an eerie knowingness; a consequence of her years spent nursing feeble old men. A cunning plan had been set in motion, and her expertise would now play a macabre role in Heis' fate.

Unfazed by his feeble protests, Anna prepared a deceptively innocent plate of spinach, its vibrant green leaves concealing a lethal secret. With a voice as smooth as silk, she assured Heis that consuming the verdant offering would restore his health. But his instincts screamed danger, a primal instinct warning him to resist. A single day later, the specter of suffering descended upon George Heis with ruthless intensity. His body succumbed to an unrelenting onslaught, and he was swiftly whisked away to the sterile confines of a hospital, teetering on the precipice of life and death. Fate had been cruel, leaving him trapped within the prison of a wheelchair for the remainder of his existence.

As George Heis reflected upon the twisted turn of events, he realized the treachery that had ensnared him. Anna, the seemingly innocuous German housewife, had concealed a wickedness that surpassed his darkest nightmares.

Oddly, George Heis didn't report Anna to the police. So, naturally, she moved onto another older man that she perceived to have money.

In early May 1937 Anna started visiting and caring for Jacob Wagner, a 78-year-old retiree who was living off a

fixed income. She managed to snake her way into Wagner's home by telling him that a relative in Germany had told her that she was related to him.

In the shadows of the quiet neighborhood, Anna's sinister plan began to unfold. With calculated precision, she approached the old man, her soft words and tender gestures weaving a web of trust around him. Little did he know that her kindness concealed a darker intention.

On that fateful evening of June 1st, Anna extended an invitation to the unsuspecting Jacob Wagner, luring him into her clutches. She meticulously prepared a sumptuous supper, carefully selecting every ingredient to ensure its potency. A glass of orange juice shimmered on the table, innocently concealing a venomous concoction that would seal his fate.

As the days passed, Jacob's health rapidly deteriorated, forcing him to be rushed to the Good Samaritan Hospital. The doctors and nurses battled to save him, unaware of the devious plot that had ensnared their patient. Meanwhile, Anna, with a twisted smile, whispered to his neighbors that her "uncle" would never return home. Morning broke, casting a pall of gloom over the neighborhood. Jacob Wagner, a mere pawn in Anna's treacherous game, breathed his last breath. But the cold embrace of death was merely the beginning of Anna's twisted gambit.

With an eerie swiftness, Anna hurried to the bank, clutching a check for $1,000, a forged gift from the deceased. She hoped to reap her ill-gotten reward, to drain the final remnants of Jacob's existence. Yet, fate had other plans. The bank manager, sensing something amiss, delved into the depths of suspicion. A few phone calls unveiled the grim truth: Jacob Wagner was dead, and Anna's deceit would not go unpunished.

But Anna, cunning and relentless, was not deterred. She knew her final triumph was yet to come. Unbeknownst to her, Jacob had left behind a testament of his twisted affection. As the estate settled, a shroud of darkness descended upon those involved. Anna, the sole beneficiary of his morbid bequest, inherited a chilling sum of $17,000, a haunting reminder of her nefarious deeds.

After Wagner's death, a friend of the deceased got the police to look into the suspicious sudden death. Once they started digging, they were intrigued by what they found.

Luella Kohler, a 79 retiree who lived in the same building as Wagner also had a run-in with Anna. After her neighbor's "niece" brought her some ice cream, she became violently ill and had to go to the hospital. While she was away being treated, someone broke into her apartment and stole several pieces of ornate jewelry. Hoping to snare another victim, Anna also tried to take some beer to Luella's 95-year-old mother, Mary Arnold. Fortunately, Mrs. Arnold refused to drink the deadly brew.

With authorities starting to pay attention, Anna got her hooks into 67-year-old retiree George Gsellman. On July 5, 1937, she invited him over to eat dinner. He was dead the next day. Hospital officials notified the authorities and the police started to pick up on the pattern.

Colorado

Oblivious to the investigations into Wagner and Gsellman's deaths, Anna moved onto the next old man she could find. After breaking one of her shoes, a friend referred her to George Obendorfer, a local cobbler. As soon as she met the 67-year-old widower, Anna turned on the charm and started talking about mountains in Europe she had seen as a child. Obendorfer fell hard for the frisky female and planned an elaborate trip to the Rocky Mountains in Colorado with the woman thirty-six years his junior.

Just a few days after they met, Obendorfer and Anna, along with her son, Oscar, were on a train to Denver. As soon as they arrived at the opulent Oxford Hotel, she eagerly prepared a simple offering of watermelon for her newfound companion.

Like a venomous serpent striking its unsuspecting prey, a vile affliction seized Obendorfer's weakened body with merciless speed. Painful dysentery coursed through his veins, transforming the once lively man into a writhing vessel of agony. Time slipped through their fingers like grains of sand in an hourglass, leaving them with a desperate race against an invisible enemy.

They managed to hop on a train for Colorado Springs but by the time they got there, the old man's health condition had worsened. When the trio reached the resort at Colorado Springs, George was knocking on death's door.

Just a few hours later, his romantic trip turned into an eternal rendezvous with the grim reaper.

After Obendorfer was pronounced dead, Anna took two of his rings, and pawned them. Though the jewelry was valued at $300, she only received $7. Almost broke with no way home, Anna contacted her husband and begged him to send money so she could buy two train tickets home. Phillip reluctantly wired his wife $30, and the next day Anna and Oscar were heading back to Ohio.

By the time Anna reached Cincinnati, the walls were starting to close in on her. After trying unsuccessfully to transfer $1,000 from Obendorfer's bank account, she was arrested and taken into custody by the police on August 11th. Initially, she was only charged with grand larceny for stealing the rings. Before she could be extradited to Colorado, Anna was charged with the murder of Jacob Wagner. Behind the scenes, detectives were scrambling to investigate the deaths of the other elderly men that she had allegedly had relationships with and cared for.

After being grilled for five hours by detectives, Anna confessed to selling the rings. According to her, they didn't belong to George Obendorfer. Her son had found them in a hotel in Colorado. Upon the discovery, Anna and her son watched the lost and found columns in local papers for a few days. Once she realized no one was looking for them, Anna decided to take the rings to a pawn shop and sell them.

Anna claimed that she was friends with Obendorfer but didn't know that he was going to Colorado. In fact, she told the officers that she was surprised to see him at the train station boarding the same train.

When the detectives began interrogating her about the deaths of the elderly men that she was caring for, Anna denied murdering anyone. She sternly told the authorities, "My conscience is clear. I have nothing to worry me."

On Trial

When Anna Marie Hahn went on trial for murder, the prosecutor dropped bomb after bomb on the defense. Not only had Anna known that George Obendorfer was going to Colorado, but the district attorney also had records that proved she had purchased his ticket. Obendorfer had also been telling friends and family that he was going out of town with a lady. Even more damning, the taxi driver that rushed Obendorfer to the hospital testified that Oscar, Anna's son, told him that George Obendorfer was very wealthy and was going to buy his mother a chicken ranch.

Jacob Wagner and George Gsellman's bodies were exhumed and found to be poisoned. After arsenic was found in Anna's purse, the D.A. had no other choice but to also charge her for their murders too.

While it was pretty obvious that the district attorney had Anna dead to rights, a wheelchair bound George Heis sealed her fate as he confronted her in front of the eleven women and one man on the jury.

Day by day, the defense's portrayal of Anna Marie Hahn, the supposed loving caregiver, began to crumble under the weight of the prosecution's evidence.

With bated breath, the prosecution produced a series of letters that would expose the true nature of this seemingly benevolent woman. As the words escaped the prosecutor's lips, they carried an unsettling weight, like whispers from the darkest corners of the human soul. These letters, once held secret, unleashed a chilling truth upon the courtroom. Anna Marie Hahn's intentions were far more sinister than anyone could have fathomed. It was a macabre dance of deception and greed, veiled behind the guise of caregiving.

In the haunting silence that followed, the letters spoke of something far more insidious. The cold ink on paper revealed a woman consumed by a voracious appetite for money.

Below is a letter to Albert Palmer.

My Dear Sweet Daddy,
I want to let you know so you won't take this trip here for nothing tomorrow. I have to go to the bank and after I get through there, I am going to stop at your house about half past eleven. I was home all day today and working hard. I'll see you tomorrow then with all my love and a lot of kisses.
Your Anna

As the trial unfolded, the gripping truth emerged, shattering the illusions of innocence that once surrounded Anna.

The sinister puzzle began to take shape, revealing a web of deception and greed. With each passing revelation, the veil of her supposed innocence was ruthlessly torn apart, leaving only a haunting darkness in its wake.

It was uncovered that years earlier, Anna had cunningly orchestrated a series of fires. With calculated precision, she had orchestrated not one, not two, but three separate blazes, ruthlessly using them as an opportunity to collect over $2,000.

But the fire insurance scheme was only the beginning of Anna's descent into darkness. With her newfound taste for ill-gotten gains, she ventured into even more sinister territory — murder.

Although it couldn't be proven, many were convinced that Anna may have poisoned her uncle, Johannes Oswald and Ernst Kohler, her former landlord. Both elderly men had left her large inheritances.

But the macabre tale did not end there. The enigmatic Anna had set her sights on another victim, her very own husband, Phillip. As the vultures of suspicion circled overhead, she made audacious attempts to secure a hefty life insurance policy, each one foiled by a twist of fate. It seemed fortune had a peculiar way of shielding Phillip from Anna's deadly grip.

Yet, fate alone could not protect Phillip forever. Like a spider lurking in the shadows, Anna toyed with her husband's life, weaving a tapestry of sickness and suffering. His health waned, teetering on the precipice of darkness, only to rebound miraculously after brief hospital stays. A sinister dance of poison and resilience played out, leaving Phillip trapped in a nightmarish cycle of uncertainty.

The catalyst for Phillip's realization came in the form of a vile discovery—a bottle of croton oil, a potent elixir of death, concealed within the confines of their home. Instinct kicked in, urging Phillip to safeguard the evidence, to unmask the insidious truth that had plagued his life.

Without the bottle, Anna had plenty of poison in the home. Police even discovered it in saltshakers in her purse! In court, Detective Chief Patrick Hayes boldly declared that Anna Han had "bought enough poison to kill half the town". Further backing up Chief Hayes' claims, scientists that were brought into exam George Gesllman's apartment found 17.94 grams of arsenic in his dish pans. Only 1.5 grams are needed to kill the average person.

In a desperate quest to obtain poison, Anna scoured the area, going to multiple pharmacists and even sending her own flesh and blood, her son, to complete the sinister transaction. But fate intervened in the form of a courageous pharmacist who refused to sell the lethal substance to a mere child.

When Anna took the witness stand, she argued that any arsenic found in her home was used for gardening. With the weight of her fate pressing down on her, she told the court that Jacob Wagner must have killed himself and insisted that she didn't create a phony will (even though a handwriting expert had debunked it on the stand). Under oath, Anna wilted under interrogation by the prosecutor and constantly kept getting tripped up with her vague and rambling answers.

The Verdict

Anna's trial lasted almost a month. The state put ninety-
six witnesses on the stand to present their case that Anna
Marie Hahn was a greedy, calculated murderess.
Astonishingly, the defense only called three. When Judge
Charles S. Bell handed things over to the jury,
surprisingly, it wasn't a slam dunk decision.

In an unexpected twist, the jury room became a
battleground of conflicting opinions. The room echoed
with heated debates and passionate arguments, as one
juror staunchly resisted the overwhelming tide of
consensus. Their defiance cast a shadow of doubt over
the proceedings, injecting an element of uncertainty into
the already charged atmosphere.

Hours turned into an eternity as the jury wrestled with
the evidence presented before them. Each piece of
information was dissected, analyzed, and scrutinized
with meticulous fervor.

But as the relentless hands of the clock pressed forward,
the weight of the evidence began to tighten its grip
around the dissident juror's wavering conviction. The
truth, like a relentless force, seeped into their mind,
chipping away at the last vestiges of doubt. Reluctantly,
they succumbed to the overwhelming weight of reason
and reluctantly fell in line with their fellow jurors.

As the judge's voice boomed across the courtroom, the
tension in the air was palpable. All eyes were fixed on

Anna, who sat motionless, her face a mask of stoicism. The sound of the gavel echoed through the room as the verdict was read out, and Anna's fate was sealed.

But as soon as the guards led her out of the courtroom, Anna's composure shattered. Running through the stark, sterile corridors of the prison, she slammed the door of her cell and collapsed onto the cold, hard floor. The weight of the guilty verdict crushed her, and she sobbed uncontrollably, her tears flowing like a river.

For what seemed like an eternity, Anna lay there, curled up in a ball as she sobbed. But eventually, she mustered the strength to pick herself up and compose a statement through her attorney. Her voice shook with emotion as she spoke, her words ringing with defiance and determination.

They have set out to get me. Now they have got me.

Naturally, Anna's attorney began the appeal process immediately. While she remained in jail, her son came to visit her each day until she was transferred to the Ohio State Penitentiary in Columbus.

Originally, Anna was scheduled to die on March 10th, 1938, but as the Ohio State Supreme Court mulled over whether to review her case, it was pushed back to December 7th.

As her case slowly maneuvered through the judicial system, Anna borrowed a typewriter from a prison secretary and started writing her life story. However, once her attorney learned of this, he went to meet with his client. Worried that media outlets who didn't receive a copy might be more inclined to view Anna unfavorably, he nixed the project. In his opinion, Anna couldn't risk any potential bad press until the courts and the governor had their say.

After the Ohio State Supreme Court dismissed the appeal, Anna's legal team made an unsuspected announcement/request. If Governor Martin L. Davey would commute Anna's sentence to life in prison, they would not seek any further appeals.

Unfortunately for the convicted murderess, the governor declined to intervene and deferred to the State Supreme Court. The day before her execution, Anna's fate was sealed, and she was left with nothing but a lengthy statement from Governor Davey, explaining his reasons for denying her plea for mercy.

The statement felt like a final blow, a crushing defeat that left Anna feeling utterly alone and abandoned. The weight of the governor's words echoed in her mind as she faced the stark reality of her imminent demise.

The Execution

The air in the room crackled with anticipation as the fateful day, December 7th, 1938, unfolded in a whirlwind of fear and desperation. Anna Marie Hahn, a woman consumed by darkness and secrets, found herself in a chilling battle against the inevitable.

Clad in blue pajamas and brown socks, a stark contrast to the fur coats she once wore, Anna was forcefully dragged from her cold, dreary cell. Her cries echoed through the prison corridors, an anguished plea for salvation in the face of impending doom. The world outside seemed oblivious to her plight, a merciless stage where justice would soon unveil its relentless face.

As Anna was led toward her grim destiny, four deputies towered over her like harbingers of doom. Each tightening strap on the electric chair felt like another shackle around her soul, binding her to the inevitable darkness that awaited. The room pulsated with an eerie energy, intensifying the growing storm within Anna's tormented mind.

A mask, black as the abyss, descended upon Anna's face, shrouding her features and obscuring the flickering flames of her haunting gaze. The world around her blurred, reduced to a claustrophobic enclosure, closing in on her final moments. Time seemed to slow, suspended in a macabre dance, as the executioners prepared to unleash the full force of mankind's retribution upon her.

Trembling with a mixture of terror and disbelief, Anna's voice pierced the silence, a desperate cry echoing through the chamber of despair. Her words, laden with desperation and a last flicker of hope, pleaded with Warden James Woodard, the final arbiter of her fate. "You can't do this to me!" she pleaded, her voice a symphony of desperation and anguish. "Won't somebody help me? Warden, don't let them do this to me!" Her pleas, a symphony of despair, reverberated through the very core of her being.

Realizing the futility of her pleas, her mind grasped onto the only solace that remained — an ancient prayer of redemption. The Lord's Prayer became her desperate battle cry, a fragile shield against the impending darkness. But time betrayed her, slipping through her trembling fingers like sand, as she couldn't even complete the sacred words before the final act of retribution unfolded.

A deafening silence filled the room, accompanied by a surge of electricity coursing through the chair, seeking out the depths of Anna's being. In that harrowing instant, as the switch was flipped, Anna's spirit was propelled into eternity and her voice was forever silenced.

After Anna became the first woman to be electrocuted in the state of Ohio, a local newspaper reached out to Phillip Hahn and asked him if he had made arrangements to claim his wife's body. Having conflicted emotions, he issued a two-word response on how he felt about the situation, "Too bad."

Confession from the Grave

Before she was executed, a writer from Cincinnati approached Anna's attorney and inquired about obtaining the rights to her confession should she choose to make one. She was made an offer of $6,000 for the exclusive story and all the funds would go into an escrow account and were to only be used for the care of her son. After spending a day or two thinking about it, Anna declined the offer.

Shortly after Anna was executed, there were whispers all around town that Anna had handed her attorney, Joseph H. Hoodin a stack of papers just before she was whisked away to the electric chair. Yet, in the days after her death, nothing was released. For nearly two weeks Cincinnati was buzzing about the rumored confession. Would she admit to the murders from the grave?

On December 19, 1938, the city got their answer. On the front page of the Enquirer was the headline, "Anna Hahn's Death Cell Confession! Four Cincinnati Murders Are Laid Bare!"

The Enquirer was able to make a deal with the murderess shortly before her execution. In return for the handwritten confession that was given to her lawyer an hour before her death, a large amount of money was set aside for the care of Anna's twelve-year-old son, Oscar.

In her own words, splashed across twenty pages that were published exclusively by the Enquirer, she brazenly admitted to the calculated murders of not one, not two, but four unsuspecting souls: Albert Palmer, George Gsellman, Jacob Wagner, and George Obendorfer. Among the glaring omissions were her uncle, Johannes Oswald and Ernst Kohler. Anna also made no mention of poisoning wheelchair bound George Heis either.

Though she claimed responsibility for four deaths, Anna hinted that possible head injuries in bicycle, skiing and ice-skating accidents as a child may have contributed to her multiple lapses in judgment.

"I know now that when I put that poison in the oysters, I wasn't in my right mind," explained Anna in the confession. "No one could do a thing like that.

I never had felt unkind to anyone and always tried to help those that were in trouble. Always I kept thinking about what I had done and why I did it.

It must have been fear for my family's future to just make me do it. Only God knows why I should have done and why I did this thing and some day He will explain what was in my mind that made me sin so."

Epilogue

A few years after Anna's execution, Phillip Hahn got remarried and spent the rest of his days living a completely normal life.

As for Oscar Hahn, once his mother's death sentence was carried out, he was placed in the care of a loving family in the Midwest. Anna's attorney, Joseph Hoodin, kept tabs on him and helped finance the young man's upbringing.

Oscar's name was legally changed, and he got to start fresh with a wonderful support situation in place. When he became of age, Arsenic Anna's son joined the navy, got married and faded away into obscurity.

Hauntings

The two-story house built in 1865 that Anna Marie Hahn obtained from Ernst Kohler was signed over to her attorney during the trial. Following her death, it was rented out for one year before being torn down.

During the year that Anna's attorney rented the place out, the people who lived there swore that the place was haunted. On the second floor, the darkness took on a life of its own. Footsteps echoed without origin, as if phantom figures roamed the hallways, their ethereal presence lingering just out of sight. Doors creaked open and shut with a mind of their own, revealing glimpses into the macabre secrets that this house had witnessed over the years.

But it was the upstairs bedrooms that became the epicenter of this supernatural nightmare. In one room, a child's long-forgotten toy came to life, defying the laws of reality. The sound of a ball bouncing echoed through the stillness, growing louder and more erratic with each passing night. The walls seemed to pulsate in rhythm, as if the very essence of the house was breathing in the despair of those who dared to stay.

The old house on Colerain that belonged to the Hahn family was torn down in 1940. After it was signed over to her attorney to pay for her legal fees, Hoodin rented it out for a year before selling the property at auction for $9,500. Today a busy convenience store is located on the site.

If you go by the location hoping to find a ghost, you are probably going to leave disappointed. According to associates, there is no paranormal activity in the building. "There are some weird things in the store," explained a longtime. "But if I'm honest, it's just the people who come in!"

Cemetery Specters

Chestnut Street Cemetery

In June 1821 prominent businessman Benjamin Lape was lying on his deathbed when he asked his family to go find two of his Jewish friends, Joseph Jonas and  Morris Moses. When the two men arrived, Benjamin confessed that he was a Jew. Regrettably, when he moved to Cincinnati, to fit into his German neighborhood, he changed his last name from Lieb to Lape. Benjamin told his friends that he was dying and requested that his Jewish brothers bury him with Jewish rites.

Jonas and Moses honored the dying man's wish and bought a small lot on the corner of Central Avenue and Chestnut Street. Benjamin Lieb became the first person laid to rest in the humble Jewish burying ground after his passing.

After cholera ravaged Cincinnati in 1849, the Chestnut Street Cemetery quickly filled up and was closed the following year.

When the Walnut Hill Jewish Cemetery opened in 1850, some families had their loved one's remains exhumed and reinterred in the new burying ground.

Over time, the cemetery was neglected and forgotten about. As the community grew up around it, developers were trying to get their hooks into the land until

successful railroad attorney Edgar Johnson stepped in. Edgar vehemently opposed any development of the sacred burial ground where his father, David had been laid to rest in 1842.

As the drama surrounding the potential development of the cemetery played out, those that lived near the Chestnut Street Cemetery claimed that they saw the Johnson patriarch sorrowfully pacing back and forth through the cemetery at night.

Edgar Johnson passed away a few years later and was buried in his family's plot in Walnut Hills. Yet, according to Cincinnati legend, his spirit could be seen with his father strolling through the old Jewish cemetery.

Spring Grove Cemetery

After cholera ravaged Cincinnati and filled up many of the graveyards, the Cincinnati Horticultural Society formed a cemetery association in 1844. The first order of business for the group was to find a site close enough to downtown so people could visit, but also have a place that wouldn't be infringed upon as the city grew.

Spring Grove Cemetery was chartered on January 21, 1845, and the first burial took place eight months later.

In 1855 acclaimed landscape architect Adolph Strauch was brought in to beautify the burial ground. His vision of a garden cemetery much like Mount Auburn in Cambridge, Massachusetts is what visitors today still find when they visit the cemetery.

With 733 acres on the property, Spring Grove Cemetery is considered to be one of the largest cemeteries in the country.

On the grounds you will find a who's who of not just Cincinnati, but the United States.

Below are just some of the notable people interned at Spring Grove Cemetery.

- Salmon Chase, Chief Justice of the United States Supreme Court

- Joseph Benson Foraker, former Ohio Governor

- William Procter and James Gamble, the founders of Procter and Gamble.

- "Fighting" Joe Hooker, Union General

- Bernard Kroger, founder of Kroger supermarkets

- Nicholas Longworth, former Speaker of the House

- Louise Taft, mother of President William Howard Taft

The Ballad of Charles Breuer

At the turn of the 20th century, Cincinnati was abuzz with rumors and whispers about the enigmatic Charles C. Breuer, a man whose wealth seemed to know no bounds. He commanded the respect and admiration of high society, his name synonymous with opulence and success. Yet, behind closed doors, a tempestuous storm was brewing, threatening to shatter the façade of his illustrious life.

Charles, having already experienced the trials and tribulations of two failed marriages, found himself captivated by the allure of his housekeeper, Georgia Lee Ghoulson. In a daring move that shocked the city's elite, he cast aside societal expectations and took Georgia as his bride in the year 1904. However, the age difference between the couple proved to be a bitter pill for some to swallow, none more so than Charles' two youngest daughters, Ruth and Helen.

Ruth, a mere twelve years old, and her slightly older sister, Helen, were deeply unsettled by their father's choice. They viewed his marriage to Georgia as a betrayal. To the young girls, it was inconceivable that their father would choose a woman twenty-five years his junior, replacing the comfortable familiarity of their mother with an unknown interloper.

Tensions mounted within the gilded walls of their luxurious mansion on Ludlow Avenue. The clash between the new matriarch and her stepdaughters became an unyielding battleground, each side fiercely defending their territory. The once harmonious household now crackled with animosity, its foundations trembling under the weight of resentment.

Unable to bear the suffocating atmosphere any longer, Ruth and Helen made a daring decision that would forever alter the trajectory of their lives. They mustered the strength to leave behind the safety and splendor of their opulent home, venturing out into the unforgiving streets of Cincinnati with nothing but the clothes on their backs. The stark reality of their newfound homelessness struck them with a brutal force, the juxtaposition of their former lives and their current destitution a harsh reminder of the price they had paid for their defiance.

Word got around town about the girls and eventually the Humane Society stepped in. The welfare organization relocated the girls into the Lawrence Home for Working Girls on Third and Broadway. Charles was summoned before a juvenile court judge and ordered to pay the girls $50 each month. ($1,700 in 2023) for support.

Although aggravated about the situation, Charles still loved his girls deeply and paid the support payments each month as ordered by the court. Nevertheless, a few years later, he became embroiled in several lawsuits after a business partner turned on him and someone fell down an elevator shaft in one of his buildings. As the legal bills piled up, Charles fell behind in his payments to his daughters.

(From left to right) Ruth, Charles and Helen Breuer

With their father not living up to his court ordered support payments, Ruth and Helen hired an attorney to get their money. Instead of going after Charles or his home, the lawyer went after one of the tycoon's biggest assets, the Franklin Building on the corner of Third and Plum Street.

The court sided with the Breuer children and appointed Union Savings Bank as the building's receiver. As part of their duties, the bank took over as the landlord and oversaw the active leases.

As the clock struck 1 o'clock, the sun cast an eerie shadow over the desolate streets of the city on that bone-chilling afternoon of January 16th, 1908. John T. Sloan, a diligent bank employee, had an ominous rendezvous awaiting him at the foreboding Franklin Building.

An angry Charles Breuer stood at the entrance of the looming structure, his eyes gleaming with a sinister glint. With a silent exchange of keys, Sloan embarked on a journey through the five-story behemoth. Each creak of the floorboards seemed to whisper a foreboding secret, intensifying the sense of impending calamity.

Step by cautious step, Sloan ventured further. The air grew heavy with anticipation, as if the walls themselves were holding their breath. Deep within the bowels of the basement, a flickering light danced before his eyes, drawing him closer with an irresistible allure.

There, amidst the suffocating darkness, Sloan stumbled upon a chilling scene — a solitary candle, its flame defiantly burning, revealing an unholy alliance with a stopper of oil. But it was the grotesque attachment at its base that made his blood turn to ice — three ominous fuses intertwined like serpents, leading to a deadly payload of four pounds of unforgiving dynamite.

A shiver raced down Sloan's spine as the gravity of the situation enveloped him. Every nerve in his body screamed of the imminent threat that loomed before him. With trembling hands and a courage he never knew he possessed, he extinguished the flame of the sinister candle.

Fear propelled him forward, his pounding footsteps echoing through the dimly lit corridors. Panic gripped his soul as he ran through the unfamiliar structure. Finally bursting through the doors of the Franklin Building, Sloan's ragged breath mingled with the frigid winter air as he scanned the bustling streets for a police officer. Without hesitation, he stumbled towards him, his words a desperate plea for help.

Initially, the police thought the bomb was a hoax and John Sloan was only playing a joke. But when a detective took the sticks of dynamite to the Austin Powder Company's plant, the explosives were deemed to be legitimate.

Within an hour or two, authorities had linked Charles Breuer to the attempted bombing and placed him under arrest. While Charles was standing on the corner waiting for the police wagon to take him to the station, an astute officer witnessed the mogul pass a gun to his wife. The policeman grabbed the weapon and hauled him off to be booked. When he arrived at the police station, Charles Breuer was charged with arson and carrying a concealed weapon.

He made bail and was released that evening.

The next day the city coroner received a letter from the accused bomber.

Dr. Otis Cameron, Coroner-Dear Sir:

My name is Charles C. Breuer, I live at 443 Ludlow Avenue. My health is good except that I have a rupture and muscular rheumatism.

I have seven children living. Some of them are spoilt and suing me for all I have for maintenance. I have married three times. The last is living with me now, but she knows nothing of what I am doing. I provided her my last will and testament December 6, A. D. 1906.

I am tired of living under our government. Consolidation means ruination. I therefore end my life tonight without the knowledge of anybody.
Your friend,
C. C. Breuer

After reading the suicide note, the coroner rushed to Ludlow Avenue to check on Charles. Strangely, when he arrived at the house, he found Charles Breuer to be very much alive. When confronted with the letter, Charles insisted that he didn't write it.

As the wacky story about the eccentric millionaire blew up in the newspapers, Charles maintained his innocence and blamed the bomb on one of his many enemies around Cincinnati. He even doubled down on his innocence and claimed that a few days earlier, an unknown assailant had fired a gun at his wife in their front yard.

When Charles had his day in court, he was deemed to be insane. The judge released him to the custody of his wife, Georgia who was appointed his guardian.

A month later, Charles was ordered back to court for a hearing. Since he was declared insane by the state, a judge had to sort through his finances and set up a trust to care for not only the aging magnate but his two youngest daughters.

Before the proceedings, as each side was milling around the courthouse, Helen Breuer, standing on one side, noticed her estranged father, Charles, across the room. Despite their strained relationship, she mustered up the courage to give him a warm, genuine smile.

Caught off guard by this unexpected gesture, Charles felt a surge of emotions welling up inside him. He couldn't hold back the floodgates any longer. Overwhelmed with regret and longing, he walked towards his daughters, trying his best to compose himself.

As Charles reached Helen and her sister, time seemed to stand still. The weight of the past and the pain they had all endured hung in the air. But in that poignant moment, as if by some miracle, the walls of resentment and hurt crumbled before their eyes.

Tears streamed down Charles' weathered face as he wrapped his arms around his precious girls. The sobs that escaped his lips were not only tears of sorrow but also tears of relief and hope. In that embrace, four long years of bitterness and misunderstandings washed away, replaced by the raw, genuine love that had always been buried deep within their hearts.

When the Breuers were called into the courtroom, the trio walked in holding hands and proceeded to sort out his affairs. Before slamming a gavel on his desk, a judge ordered that all of Charles Breuer's holdings in Clifton, Avondale and Brighton were to be auctioned. Once the pending lawsuits were settled, the proceeds of the sale were designated for the daughters as well as the care of the Breuer patriarch.

Though Charles Breuer had his pride and identity stripped away by the judge, he had a smile on his face as he walked out of the courtroom surrounded by his wife and daughters.

I wish I could end the story here with a happy ending. Sadly, there's more to the story.

Unlike most people who get in trouble and plead insanity to get out of jail, Charles Breuer really had started going insane.

Charles went missing on the Fourth of July, but days later turned up at the Eighth District Police Station demanding to be protected. According to him, there were people he had done business with that wanted to kill him. Charles was taken home to his wife, but he left again a few days later. He was found walking the railroad tracks near

Galion, Ohio mumbling to himself. Once again, Charles was brought home, but he wouldn't be there long.

On July 11th an officer on patrol heard someone yelling at the Breuer home. When he knocked on the door, he was greeted by a badly bruised Charles Breuer. In the background the policeman heard Georgia Breuer screaming and begging for help. The officer burst inside and was immediately tackled and subdued by the senile old man. Fortunately, five other officers rushed into the mansion and pulled Charles off and hauled him to jail.

Georgia Breuer knew she couldn't handle her husband, but she asked the court to allow her to send him to a private asylum in California where he could be treated. But due to Charles' volatility and aggression, a judge ordered that he be sent to Longview Asylum.

He wasn't there long. Charles Breuer died on August 20th. As he drew his last breath, Charles was surrounded by his wife and two daughters.

Today Charles Breuer's grave marker is one of the most peculiar in the historic cemetery. While there are lots of extravagant headstones at Spring Grove, Charles' marker in section 100 is a little unnerving when you look at it closely. When the marker was created, the company that created his bust inserted glass eyes. Some claim that the eyes follow you as you walk around the cemetery.

There are many stories about Charles Breuer and his marker. According to a debunked Cincinnati legend, he was an optometrist who wanted his eyes preserved after his death and placed in his bust overlooking his grave.

It's easy to poke holes in this urban legend since the eyes would've decomposed a long, long time ago had they been real.

But why are the glass eyes there? No one knows for sure, but it's been speculated that Charles wanted to give the impression that he was literally keeping an eye on his family from beyond the grave.

In case you were wondering, neither Helen nor Ruth are buried in the family plot with their father. Though the girls reconciled with the dad, Helen later got married and moved away to Nashville. She is buried there. Ruth also got married years later and was laid to rest in Symmes Township.

St. Joseph Cemetery

Located at the intersection of West Eighth Street and Seton Avenue in Price Hill, you will find St. Joseph Cemetery.

Consecrated in 1843, the 128-acre burying ground was originally a German Catholic cemetery. In fact, as you walk around and marvel at some of the old grave markers, you will find that the majority of the inscriptions are done in German.

Over the years St. Joseph Cemetery has evolved and now accepts Catholics from all nationalities and backgrounds.

The Headless Horror

After the death of Joseph Nagel in 1881, his loved ones made the decision to reinter all his immediate family in one large plot in section 13.

George Meiner, a sexton along with three other grave diggers were tasked with digging up the remains of Joseph's mother, Vital Nagel. Mrs. Nagel had originally been interred in an older section of the cemetery in 1876.

The day the Nagel matriarch was to be exhumed; a handful of family members came to oversee the morbid process. As the gravediggers dug a few feet down into the soil, one of the men struck something hard and everyone stopped digging. Thinking that they had found Mrs. Nagel's casket, the men carefully began pulling the soil away. Oddly, as they pulled the dirt up, the grave diggers quickly realized that they hadn't found the coffin; they had found Vital Nagel.

When Mrs. Nagel was laid to rest, the family had little money and buried her in a shallow grave without a casket. In her five years underground in St. Joseph Cemetery, Mrs. Nagel's body didn't decompose. It did the opposite; it petrified and became as hard as a rock!

The four gravediggers tried with all their might to lift the marble statue-like cadaver from the grave but couldn't get it to budge. Thinking on his feet, sexton George Meiner started striking Mrs. Nagel's arms with his pick. If he could just break off the deceased's appendages, surely, they would be able to move her to a new resting place near her son. As the ungodly spectacle played out, some of the offended family members on hand ran screaming out of the cemetery. Meiner's efforts were for naught, as Mrs. Negley's arms and legs could not be removed.

Eventually word spread around the neighborhood and more of the Nagel family arrived at the burying ground with straps. After Mrs. Negley's body was secured, it took nearly a dozen men to pull her remains from the grave.

However, as they were bringing the woman to the surface, a pick propped up against her headstone fell over and landed flush with her neck. At that moment, Mrs. Negley's head broke off and rolled off into her grave. Aghast at the terrifying site, the remaining family

members fled the cemetery as Meiner clumsily fished the head out with his shovel. Within the hour, she was laid to rest again with her son and husband in the family plot nearby.

Singing Specters

In the dim hours of the 19th century, John Lowry, the sexton of St. Joseph Cemetery, found himself immersed in an unsettling realm. Dwelling amidst the tombstones and grave markers, he often heard a haunted melody that whispered through the air. The lifeless figures beneath the soil seemed to awaken, their spectral voices mingling in a ghostly symphony.

Amidst the solemn graves, echoes of innocent laughter cascaded through the night, their source concealed by the veil of eternity. Conversations, once meant for the living, now echoed from the deceased, as they exchanged secrets and whispered tales of the graveyard's secrets. Though the eerie correspondence initially unsettled the weathered caretaker, the spectral discourse became his somber companion, a twisted harmony that gradually seeped into his soul.

The bizarre story about the sexton that heard unbelievable sounds in the cemetery circulated around town until it was reported in a local newspaper in 1892.

I've been in St. Joseph Cemetery on a handful of occasions, but I have yet to hear any of the dead conversing with each other.

Forgotten Phantoms

The Ghost in the Engine House

In the late 19th century, the Hall family was a pillar of the Cincinnati Fire Department. Will Hall served the department with distinction as a lieutenant and his brother, "Big" John Hall was a member of Company No. 18 on Eastern Avenue.

Standing over 6' tall and weighing 250 pounds, John was not only a large man, but he had a reputation for being a brawler who often went looking for trouble. Though Big John never lost a fight, eventually he left the rough and tumble lifestyle behind. Once his sister died and he was left raising his two young nieces, John Hall settled down, got married and had six children of his own. With a large family to provide for, he became a firefighter like his brother.

Sadly, in 1890, John developed bladder problems and his health began to deteriorate. With no appetite, the once imposing figure lost over one hundred pounds. Rapidly becoming a liability for the fire department, Will Hall helped his brother get transferred to Engine Company 25 in West End where things were a little slower.

Despite an easier workload, John got some bad news in the summer of 1893. Nothing was working and doctors told him that the issue with his bladder would eventually kill him.

Knowing the end was near, John fell into a funk and began to withdraw from friends and family. With his morale at an all-time low, John's close friend and Secretary of the Fire Trustees, Tom Brown, passed away on November 4th. Like other firemen, John went to the service at the Elks' Hall two days later to pay his respects. After the funeral, a large contingent of fire fighters decided to head over to Gift's Engine House on Sixth Avenue to mingle and celebrate the life of their fallen brother.

As the heavy scent of smoke and camaraderie filled the air in the crowded firehall, John's entrance seemed to inject a burst of vibrant energy into the room. With a lit cigar dangling from his lips, he engaged in animated conversations, sharing laughter and stories with his comrades. But beneath that façade of mirth, a shadow lurked in John's eyes, unnoticed by the jubilant crowd.

As the evening wore on, an invisible force tugged at John, pulling him away from the revelry and into the depths of the firehall. Downstairs, in the dimly lit basement, his footsteps echoed against the cold, damp walls. It was there that he unexpectedly encountered his long-time friend, Yank Webb, amidst the tools and machinery of the workshop.

"Hello, Big John!" Yank's voice boomed, a mix of surprise and delight, reverberating through the confined space. But John paid no heed to the familiar greeting. He brushed past his bewildered friend, a tempest of emotions brewing within him, and slammed shut the heavy door of the water closet.

Confused and concerned, Yank stood alone, wondering what was wrong with his old pal. Pushing open the creaking door, Yank ascended the stairs and proceeded to join the festivities.

Suddenly, piercing through the raucous celebration above, a single gunshot exploded like thunder, shattering the air with its lethal intent. Time ground to a halt as Yank's heart pounded in his chest, a primal fear seizing hold of him. Instinct propelled him back down the stairs and into the small bathroom.

There, bathed in a sickly pool of crimson, lay John, his lifeblood seeping from a harrowing wound to his temple. The stench of gunpowder hung heavy in the air, intermingling with the acrid tang of regret. A .38 revolver lay abandoned on the ground, a mute witness to the tragedy that had unfolded.

In the face of unimaginable pain and despair, Big John fought valiantly against the cold grasp of death. With every shallow breath, every flicker of fading consciousness, he defied the odds, embodying the unyielding spirit that had made him a legendary figure among his peers. Time stretched out agonizingly, as if fate itself grappled with the decision of when to release him.

Sadly, the husband and father of six eventually succumbed to the self-inflicted wound.

After John was pronounced dead, a doctor found a handwritten suicide note written a few days earlier in one of his pockets.

Cincinnati, November 4, 1893

My Dear Wife: This being my last day on earth, and it being the last request I can make of you, and it is this: that you take good care of my dear children and treat them kindly, and also be kind to my sister's children, Carrie and Lotta Miller, and they have no one but me to look to, and that is my last request, and would like for this pistol which I kill myself with to go to my son, John Hall.

I left my overcoat at Schulthesiss' saloon on Vine Street. Mary, I have doctored so much that I have got tired and sore and can't help what I am going to do now. Now Mary, may God forgive me for taking what he gave me. And all pray for me.

Goodbye, my dear wife and children. This is my last request, and it is that Mr. Perkins, Fire Commissioner, he is entrusted with the charge of my estate that being my last request so help me God.

John Hall

After the death of his old friend, Yank's world turned eerie and unsettling. The Engine House, once a place of camaraderie and bravery, now seemed haunted by an invisible presence. Yank, torn between his sense of duty as a fireman and the growing unease within him, couldn't bring himself to abandon the station.

One fateful day, as Yank toiled away in his workshop downstairs, the air grew thick with tension. Suddenly, a familiar voice pierced through the silence, echoing his name, "Oh Yank!" His heart raced, and he shot up from his chair, searching desperately for the source of the prank. But to his bewilderment, the engine house stood empty, devoid of any living soul.

Doubt gnawed at Yank's mind, shrouding his thoughts in a veil of uncertainty. Was grief playing tricks on him? The following evening, as Yank descended the stairs once more, he hoped for respite from the torment. Everything appeared normal, and the silence offered a fleeting solace. But the calm was short-lived.

In the dead of night, Yank's ears were besieged by a haunting call. The voice, so unmistakably that of Big John, resonated through the hollow corridors, seeping into his very soul. His dead pal seemed to be reaching out from beyond the grave, seeking solace or perhaps delivering a message. Yet, the unnerving encounters didn't confine themselves to the nocturnal hours. Even in broad daylight, Yank could hear the echoes of his friend's voice, whispering to him.

Driven to the edge of sanity, Yank Webb made a decision borne out of desperation. He couldn't bear the spectral torment any longer. With a heavy heart, he approached his captain, seeking a transfer to another fire station. At first, his plea was met with dismissive laughter, as his captain brushed off the supernatural claims. But Yank's persistence and unwavering determination eventually wore down the captain's skepticism.

Relief flooded over Yank when he received permission to relocate. His escape from the haunted Engine House felt like a second chance at his career.

Today the old Gift's Engine House is all but a memory. In 1917, the old firehouse was acquired by the Greenwood Realty Company. The building was extensively remodeled and turned into a 1,100-seat theater.

In 1946 the property was sold again, and the theater was razed. The following year the site became the home of the Terrace Plaza Hotel.

The hotel remained in operation until 2008 when it was finally shut down. Sadly, the space is still sitting empty today. Perhaps Big John likes the peace and quiet of the vacant spacious building.

The Scalded Spirit

In the ominous evening of October 13, 1887, Julius Sutter braved the eerie corridors of the Jung Brewery, his mind heavy with fatigue. Little did he know that the shadows concealed a terrifying fate awaiting him. As he descended into the heart of the brewery, the relentless grip of darkness tightened its hold.

With his lantern casting trembling shadows on the ancient pipes, Julius meticulously examined the massive boilers. Suddenly, an ominous creak resonated through the air, followed by a bone-chilling hiss. A burst pipe, fueled by malevolent forces, unleashed its scalding wrath upon the unsuspecting worker.

Agony consumed Julius as his flesh was instantly branded by the merciless touch of searing heat. In a desperate plea for salvation, his anguished cries pierced the stillness, resonating through the labyrinthine halls. But hope materialized in the form of a vigilant comrade, whose ears caught the echoes of Julius' torment.

Summoning all his strength, the valiant co-worker raced to the rescue and dragged the tortured soul from the clutches of the malevolent boiler room. Their escape, though brief, felt like a respite from the jaws of certain doom.

But fate, cruel and merciless, had already cast its grim verdict. The dawn of the following day brought no reprieve, only a somber reminder of the irrevocable tragedy that had unfolded. Consumed by the relentless burn of his injuries, Julius Sutter succumbed to the relentless grasp of the afterlife.

Word soon spread among the brewery employees, whispers that carried the weight of the supernatural. In the dead of night, while the world slumbered in blissful ignorance, those working late shifts claimed to hear ethereal footsteps echoing through the desolate corridors. The sound, faint yet distinct, seemed to emanate from the long-forgotten boiler room where Julius had met his tragic end.

As if that weren't spine-tingling enough, some of the braver souls among the employees insisted that they had caught glimpses of Julius himself, his ghostly figure wandering the dimly lit halls. A translucent specter, trapped between the realms of the living and the dead, haunting the very place he had once toiled with sweat and determination.

News of the ghostly encounters soon permeated the city, saturating every saloon and tavern with tales of the brewery's haunted past. Curiosity morphed into obsession, and local reporters, eager to uncover the truth behind the spectral legend, descended upon the brewery like vultures drawn to a carcass.

While some staff members were skittish about talking about ghosts with the press, night fireman Frank Stumpf agreed to be interviewed by the Enquirer. When asked if he had seen the ghost of Julius Sutter, Stumpf emphatically insisted that he had.

"I have indeed," declared Stumpf, who was a friend of Julius Sutter. "Oh, you may laugh but it is true. There is no hoax about this either. I saw Sutter just as plainly as though he were still working about the boiler room.

It may strike you as mighty strange. It did me. I know.

Between twelve and one o'clock last Monday night I had occasion to go into the boiler room. I was in that room Sutter was brought and seated upon a pair of steps after he was scalded. The room is the one from which water is fed to the boilers, and I went into see how the water was running. I had got into the room and closed the door behind me."

In the early 20th century, the Jung Brewery was torn down and a school was built on the site. Today, the school sits empty waiting to be redeveloped and Julius Sutter has the place to himself.

The Sans Souci Specter

In the 1830s, amidst the shadows that embraced Third Street, there stood a place known as The Sans Souci, a den of vice and gambling that beckoned the lost souls of dock workers and riverboat crews. Within its tainted walls, a fateful night unraveled, casting a malevolent veil over the establishment.

It was during a tumultuous game of poker that William Paden, a weathered steamboat captain, succumbed to greed's seductive whispers. Seizing an audacious opportunity, he snatched a princely sum of $1,000, a fortune in those desolate times, and attempted a hasty escape through the doors of The Sans Souci.

But the wrath of the damned is relentless. As the stolen currency slipped through his fingers, an inferno of retribution was ignited. Like savages, the wretched souls within the gambling house pursued Captain Paden through the dimly lit streets, their frenzy echoing through the night. Their relentless assault silenced the captain's last breath, leaving him lifeless upon the cold, unforgiving pavement.

Days later, a servant ascended the creaking stairs that led to the gambling hall, bearing witness to a sight that would haunt his very existence. Frozen in terror, he stumbled upon the ethereal figure of Captain Paden himself. The captain clutched a handful of spectral gold coins, his spectral gaze piercing the servant's very soul, as if beckoning him to partake in a game of chance. With every ounce of sanity shattered, the servant fled, never to return to that malefic abode.

A month or so later, two dock workers got into a fist fight over a game of cards. As tables and chairs went flying during the fisticuffs, out of nowhere, Captain Paden appeared. The steamboat captain was holding a large bowie knife and had a menacing scowl on his face. The two men fighting stopped dead in their tracks and ran out of the gambling hall along with everyone else in the room.

On another occasion, two deck hands were playing poker late one evening. When they finished their hand, an old haggard man sat down at the table and said, "Deal me in, boys!" Puzzled, the dealer asked, "Who are you?" The mysterious traveler gave him an odd look and then shouted, "I'm old Cap Paden, ha, ha, ha, ha!" before slowly fading.

Word spread around town about the ghost in the gambling hall. It wasn't too long before every person who worked along the Ohio River heard about it too. People stopped coming to The Sans Souci and within a few months, the owner reluctantly was forced to close the doors.

Cincinnati Music Hall

The Invisible Killer

As Cincinnati became one of the fastest growing cities in the United States in the mid-19th century, the town found itself with a menacing invisible threat that was wreaking havoc on other port cities like New Orleans and Louisville. In 1833 cholera quietly made its way into Cincinnati and killed 3,000 people that spring and summer. In all, 2% of the city's population died from the deadly viral infection. Many of them were taken to a pauper's burying ground on the northern outskirts of town and buried.

Death lurked in every sip of water, an invisible assassin waiting to strike without mercy. In a twisted game of chance, it mattered not one's wealth or social standing— riches crumbled, colors blurred. The lethal bacteria, a malevolent force, invaded the innocent fruits and tainted springs, spreading its venomous grip. Survival, a mere coin flip, hung in the balance during those dreadful first hours. The affliction showed no mercy, claiming the lives of eminent doctors, slaves, and free souls alike, their bodies tormented by violent anguish and a torturous demise.

But after an emphasis was placed on quarantine procedures at the ports, the ravaging plague relinquished its grip, retreating into the shadows from whence it came.

Nevertheless, in 1849, the lethal bacteria returned to the United States with a vengeance claiming the life of

President James K. Polk in June, just two months after he left the White House.

Like Nashville where Polk was living, Cincinnati was also struggling with cleanliness along its dirty docks. Due to thousands of people coming in and out of town each day and poor sanitation, Cincinnati was a perfect breeding ground for cholera.

Cincinnati Riverfront 1860

Once again, the bacteria got into the drinking water and killed 6,000 of the 115,000 people in the Queen City. In fact, at the time, Cincinnati had more deaths than New York and Philadelphia combined! Again, more and more bodies were hastily buried in pauper's graves in what was becoming known as Over-the-Rhine in North Cincinnati.

Due to all the death and despair in town, people left in droves and fled to places like Mt. Healthy where they believed they would be safer from the invisible killer.

At the time Cincinnati was the sixth largest city in the country, but it was also the dirtiest. Local officials hadn't yet linked cholera to bad drinking water, but John Lea, a local geologist did make the connection. Going door to door, he figured out that families who boiled their water or drank rainwater from cisterns were not getting sick. In one neighborhood consisting of nineteen homes along Sycamore Street, Lea linked 44 deaths to a tainted spring where all of those who died got their water.

Once the cholera scare had subsided, Cincinnati put a renewed emphasis on cleanliness at the docks as well as privies and outhouses. Sewers were diverted and pigs that used to roam free and eat trash were no longer allowed in the streets.

Cholera would flare up again in 1866 and 1873 but fortunately city leaders were able to get a grasp on it early on and only a small percentage of the population died.

Blood Fell from the Sky

The night was filled with anticipation as the majestic steamboat Moselle prepared for its daring journey to St. Louis. Cincinnati's proud creation, this vessel was a symbol of unrivaled speed and power, capable of conquering the mighty river currents with ease.
On that fateful evening of April 25, 1838, over three hundred souls embarked on the Moselle, unaware of the heart-stopping events that would soon unfold.

With a resounding roar, the Moselle's steam-powered engines thundered to life, propelling the vessel away from the safety of the dock. Captain Isaac Perrin, a man of audacious ambition, yearned to prove the might of his ship, determined to outshine a rival vessel that had taken off earlier that day. His obsession for victory had led him to push his beloved steamboat to its very limits.

As the Moselle ventured down the river, a looming danger lurked within its bowels. Excess steam, like a raging tempest, surged through the ship's boilers, causing concern among the crew. Yet, Captain Perrin, consumed by his insatiable desire for speed, dismissed the warnings, recklessly demanding more power from his reluctant engineer. In the fading light of dusk, the steamboat made an unexpected detour, backtracking to the Fulton shipyard to gather additional passengers.

Tensions mounted as the ship's engineer confronted Captain Perrin, expressing his fears about the dangerously high pressure within the boilers. But the captain's fierce determination clashed with reason, and their heated exchange ended in defiance as the engineer stormed off, leaving behind a cloud of uncertainty.

Undeterred by the disagreement, Captain Perrin set his sights on the horizon, pushing the Moselle forward with unwavering resolve. The ship sliced through the water, its engines straining against the currents, as the night grew darker and more foreboding. Suddenly, a deafening blast shattered the tranquility of the river. In a cataclysmic display of destruction, all four boilers on the Moselle erupted simultaneously.

A blinding inferno engulfed the vessel, casting a hellish glow across the river, its fury visible for miles. The blast sent shockwaves through the air, ripping apart the ship's once proud structure.

Bodies were flung through the air, torn apart by the merciless force of the explosion. Limbs and debris  rained down upon the shores of Ohio and Kentucky, painting a macabre scene of shattered dreams and shattered lives. Panic swept through the survivors; their screams of terror swallowed by the night as they desperately clung to the fragments of their shattered reality.

According to the Cincinnati Whig, "Heads, limbs, bodies and blood, were seen flying through the air in every direction, attended by the most horrible shrieks and groans from the wounded and dying."

The explosion was so intense that pieces of the boilers were found 400 yards from the site. Captain Perrin's body was found later that night on the shore.

Panic and desperation seized the air as the news spread like wildfire through the city. Thousands of horrified onlookers, their hearts pounding in their chests, flocked to the river's edge, drawn by a haunting spectacle that would forever be etched into their memories. The once serene riverfront now resembled a gruesome battlefield, strewn with the shattered remnants of human bodies.

Arms, legs, and torsos lay scattered haphazardly, a chilling mosaic of devastation. The stench of death hung heavy in the air, mingling with the cries of anguished souls desperately searching for survivors.

Amid the chaos, a brave soul dared to venture into the treacherous waters, driven by an instinct to help those in need. With each step, their heart sank deeper, as the magnitude of the tragedy became all too apparent. Sixty lifeless forms bobbed silently, a macabre dance with the merciless current.

Yet, hope flickered dimly amidst the tragedy. Against all odds, a few souls emerged from the treacherous depths, gasping for breath and clinging to life. Their battered bodies and haunted eyes bore witness to the horrors they had endured. But their survival, a cruel twist of fate, only added to their torment.

As the survivors stumbled ashore, their trembling limbs gave way beneath them, robbed of strength by the weight of unspeakable grief. The realization crashed upon them like a tidal wave, shattering their fragile spirits. Their loved ones, their anchors in this chaotic world, were lost forever.

Innocent children, their tear-streaked faces etched with a sorrow far beyond their years, wailed in despair. Their dreams shattered, their futures uncertain, they clung to one another, seeking solace in the midst of unimaginable loss. Orphaned in an instant, their world turned upside down, they faced an uncertain path fraught with pain and loneliness.

A father, clutching his rescued son, was devastated to discover his wife and five daughters had perished. Overwhelmed by the tragic sight, he collapsed by the river, tears streaming, pleading for the reaper's mercy to end his unbearable anguish.

In all, 160 known people died that night. However, there were roughly two dozen passengers who didn't register and remain uncounted and unaccounted for. In reality, the death count was likely closer to 180.

Like those that perished from cholera six years earlier, the remains of those killed were rounded up and hurriedly buried in the potter's field on the north side of town.

From the Pest House to the Exposition Hall

From the 1830s until the mid-19th century, the old pauper's graveyard became home to an orphanage and the city pest house. Those who had been diagnosed with cholera, smallpox and tuberculosis were sent to the pest house to be isolated from the general population. Unlike a hospital, no treatment was given; they were sent there to die! After they passed away, their remains were taken outside and buried in a shallow grave amongst the other unknowns who had quietly been laid to rest years later.

According to Joseph Emery, a city missionary, in 1852 there were 1,800 graves in the potter's field.

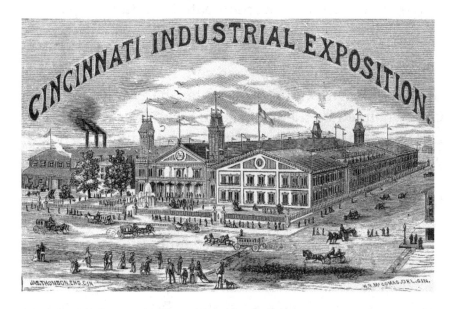

A decade or two later, Sangerhalle, a building for German singing festivals was built on the site. A few years later, wings were added, and the site became known as the Cincinnati Exposition Hall.

The sprawling wooden structure was 250′ long, 110′ wide and had an 80′ ceiling. The building was home to industrial expositions, horticulture displays and most importantly, German song festivals. When the second May Festival was held in 1875, a violent storm blew into Cincinnati. As hail loudly beat against the tin roof and water started to pour into the building, conductor Theodore Thomas abruptly had to take an intermission.

One of the men present that day that left soaking wet was Reuben Springer. Having made a fortune as a grocery wholesaler, Springer put his money where his mouth was and pledged $125,000 for a new modern music hall. But there was one caveat, in order to get the money, the citizens of Cincinnati would have to match him. 386 other prominent people in the community stepped up and matched Springer's donation. The old Exposition Hall was razed in 1876 and crews started preparing the land for the new music hall.

According to those in the community, the old Exposition Hall was believed to either be cursed or haunted depending on who you talked to. In the six years the building was in operation, the Cincinnati fire department had to put out seventy-six different fires.

For those more inclined to believe in the paranormal, there were some ghost stories as well. According to an article in the Cincinnati Commercial, a former nightwatchman experienced a lot of odd things after the sun went down that he could never explain.

"The weirdest and strangest noises would occur at intervals all night," claimed the officer. "Rappings on the ceiling, under the floor, on the doors and windows, the sound of stealthy footfalls behind me, or of loud tramping before me; the crash of heavy timbers thrown from the ceiling, of glass dashed upon the floor, of heavy bodies being dragged over the planking, these never ceased except during Exposition time."

In the midst of a relentless winter snowstorm, the watchman's heart pounded with anticipation as a deafening knock reverberated through the desolate Exposition Hall. Eager to offer solace to a weary traveler seeking refuge from the bitter cold, he swung open the heavy doors, only to confront an eerie void. His blood ran cold as he realized there were no footprints in the snow, defying all logic and reason.

The knocks at the door got to be so frequent that the watchman tuned them out. In fact, when people actually came and knocked on the door, he wouldn't let them in.

"They never annoy me now by mere knocking and rapping, for I have got used to it," explained the watchman. "I'm so used to it that sometimes when people have really knocked at the door I didn't open, because I thought it was only the dead that kept knocking, knocking, knocking."

The Music Hall

Samuel Hannaford was hired to design a new High Victorian Gothic structure that would become Cincinnati's new Music Hall. Once the cornerstone was laid in 1877, workers got busy building the gargantuan building on Elm Street.

One year and over a million bricks later, the new building was finally complete and open to the public. The following year, Industrial Hall, the north wing and Horticultural Hall, the south wing were added for exposition and convention space.

Through the years notable entertainers such as Luciano Pavarotti, Duke Ellington, Benny Goodman and Frank Sinatra have all performed at the Music Hall.

In addition to music, other notable events such as basketball, ice skating, professional wrestling, roller

 derby and boxing have been held in the Industrial Hall over the years. But the north hall wasn't just for sporting events. Full-size homes were constructed in the north hall during the Home Beautiful Expositions from 1925 to 1936. Visitors to the trade show could place orders and an identical home would be built for them on a lot in town.

Today you aren't going to find the WWE running a show in the Music Hall. But the building is still home to the Cincinnati Symphony Orchestra, the Cincinnati Pops, the Cincinnati Ballet and the Cincinnati Opera.

Where the Bodies are Buried

As you would expect, a number of skeletons have been found on the site of the Music Hall. In fact, as it was being built, hundreds of bones were discovered. City leaders decided to put the remains into eighteen boxes and bury them at Spring Grove Cemetery.

When the Music Hall was being renovated in the 1920s even more remains were discovered on the site. On June 30, 1928, the American Wreckage and Salvage Company unearthed 207 pounds of bones which were believed to belong to sixty-five people who had been interred in the potter's field years earlier.

As crews worked on the building, bones were literally found every day from June until the project was completed in September.

Oddly, a few of the nineteen skulls found on the property came up missing but after an expert was brought in; he claimed that the skulls hadn't been stolen. In his expert opinion, the old brittle bone turned to dust and blew away!

Adding to the unnerving scene, workers stumbled upon fragments of coffins and an ominous coin bearing the date 1811. As if beckoning from beyond the grave, a solitary headstone materialized, bearing the name of George Pollock—a Scottish immigrant who met his demise on October 29, 1831, at the age of 52. These grim artifacts whispered tales of a forgotten past, enveloping the construction site in an atmosphere of palpable terror.

On September 28, 1928, all the bones that were found during the renovations were reburied under an elevator shaft in the south wing of the Music Hall.

By 1988 the remains under the elevator shaft had long been forgotten when crews accidentally found them during another renovation. The bones were turned over to the University of Cincinnati to be studied. Once the school was done with them, the bones were buried in Spring Grove Cemetery.

Eighteen years later, even more remains were found at the Music Hall underneath the orchestra pit. When experts came in to test the soil under the building for asbestos, they discovered bones buried under a few inches of dirt.

Around that same time a new parking garage and convention center were added. Guess what they found as they were being built?

You guessed it. Even more bones!

Hauntings

Legend has it that the Music Hall, much like its predecessor, the infamous Exposition Hall, is a hotbed of supernatural activity. Within those hallowed halls are lurking restless spirits trapped in a spectral symphony of the unknown. Shadows dancing and twisting, taunting the living with their elusive presence. It is said that the very air within the building holds an otherworldly energy, thick with the echoes of the past.

Judy Knuckles of Cincinnati Research and Paranormal Studies has had her fair share of unique experiences in the building. In addition to leading ghost tours in the Music Hall, she and her team have held investigations in the historic structure.

"There are so many stories," exclaimed Knuckles. "One night my niece and I were sitting on the stage during an investigation. We looked up in the gallery and saw a shadow of a man walk in the door and walk down the back aisle. About halfway across, he just disappeared!"

In the depths of the Music Hall's history, whispers echo of more than just men. Legends tell of a ghostly woman, shrouded in mystery, haunting the very halls where she was likely buried. Her ethereal presence lingers, unseen yet felt, as she traverses the ancient corridors of this hallowed venue.

For over three decades, Erich Kunzel stood as the unyielding maestro of the Cincinnati Pops, mastering the symphonies that resonated within those hallowed walls. Little did he know that the mysterious lady was waiting to unveil her ethereal presence.

In the depths of the night, as silence blanketed the empty concert hall, an eerie melody would pierce the air, like a ghostly siren's call. It was the haunting voice of a woman, her ethereal song reverberating through the vast expanse. Kunzel would stand in awe, his heart pounding, as he strained to discern the source of the spectral serenade. Yet, as he ventured closer to the stage, the singing would abruptly cease, leaving nothing but an enigmatic void.

Undeterred, Kunzel's unwavering curiosity drove him deeper into the labyrinthine secrets of the Music Hall. Among the shadows of the gallery, he would catch fleeting glimpses of a young boy, ethereal and enigmatic.

The child's gaze held a timeless longing, hinting at a life cut short and a destiny unresolved. It was a phantom presence that sent chills down the spines of all who encountered it.

Word of the otherworldly inhabitants spread like wildfire among the concertgoers, an air of anticipation mingling with trepidation. Those who ventured into the Music Hall's sacred halls would find themselves in the company of specters from a bygone era. The spirits would materialize in fleeting moments, casting ghostly apparitions amidst the rows of empty seats, a chilling reminder of the enduring power of the past.

"I remember coming to see the symphony a few years ago," recalled Jessica Bright. "As I was about to sit down, I saw a little boy wearing older clothes. He really stood

out because everyone there was dressed so nicely. But that boy looked like he didn't belong there.

When my husband and I took our seats, I leaned over to get his attention. Before I could even ask him if he saw the little boy, the kid was gone! I had heard that the Music Hall was haunted but that was enough to really convince me!

I went back once or twice after that, but I never saw the little boy again."

"There are lots of stories about children in the building," explained Judy Knuckles. "That's where the orphanage used to be! One time when my niece was in the basement, she clearly saw a pair of little legs from the thigh down run behind a symphony case that was down there."

In addition to the apparitions, cold spots have occasionally been detected in the building, usually in one particular spot.

According to those who work in the Music Hall, within the hallowed walls is a place that holds a literal chilling secret. On the second floor of the foyer, there is a certain place where the temperature has been known to rapidly change. Whether it is in the scorching heat of July or the sweltering days of August, the temperature will suddenly drop forty degrees and anyone who walks through it will experience an icy chill.

The enigmatic temperature shift was attributed to the spirits' ethereal journeys, their very essence intertwining with the physical realm. As they traversed the boundaries of existence, they drew upon the energy of their surroundings, leaving behind a frigid trail in their wake.

The Lady in Green

During the challenging era of the Great Depression in the 1920s and 1930s, a remarkable enthusiasm for skyscrapers gripped the United States. The monumental presence of iconic structures like the Tribune Tower in Chicago and the Empire State Building in New York City inspired a fervor for constructing grand multistory buildings across the nation. Against this backdrop, Cincinnati emerged as a city ready to embrace the trend and embark on its own ambitious endeavor to erect a supersized skyscraper.

On August 24, 1929, it was announced that a large complex anchored by a 49-story skyscraper bounded by Vine, Race and Fifth Streets would be erected in downtown Cincinnati. A new office building called the Carew Tower would be built alongside a $7 million dollar 28-story hotel. A shopping center and a parking garage were also incorporated into the designs making the sprawling 1.3 million square foot mixed-use commercial development a city within a city.

Upon its completion in 1931, the Carew Tower project boasted an impressive complex composed of various elements. The edifice incorporated a staggering 4,000,000 bricks, 8,000 windows, 5,000 doors, and an astounding 60 miles of floor and window molding. Additionally, it required the installation of 37 miles of steel pipe, 15,000 tons of structural steel, 40 railroad cars worth of stone, 15 railroad cars filled with glass, and an impressive 60 railroad cars filled with lumber.

The Carew Tower was the largest building in Cincinnati until the Great American Tower was built in 2010. Originally, the opulent hotel onsite was named the St. Nicholas Plaza in honor of the old St. Nicholas Hotel that operated on the southeast corner of Fourth and Race Streets from 1888 to 1911. However, shortly after the new hotel was incorporated, the owners found out that they had a problem. Even though the St. Nicholas Hotel had gone out of business, the Cincinnati Realty Company owned the rights to the hotel's name. Seeing an opportunity to make a few bucks in a lawsuit, the real estate company requested an injunction and asked that the St. Nicholas Plaza be renamed.

The owners of the new hotel balked and argued that the Cincinnati Realty Company had abandoned their intellectual property since they had not used it in twenty years. Nevertheless, when the two businesses went before the court, Judge Stanley Struble sided with the Cincinnati Realty Company.

The owners of the St. Nicholas Plaza found themselves in a bind. Despite the hotel being already open, they were facing a significant challenge. They had invested a substantial amount, a staggering half a million dollars, in acquiring various items for the hotel's operation. These included 100,000 pieces of delicate china, 11,133 pieces of exquisite holloware, 72,383 pieces of elegant silverware, 10,800 meticulously crafted napkins, 3,000 high-quality tablecloths, 2,000 bedspreads, 8,500 plush towels, 2,500 bathmats, and 750 employee uniforms. Remarkably, each of these items bore the distinguished mark of *St. NP*, either meticulously stamped or elegantly embroidered onto them.

A few days after the St. Nicholas Plaza's grand opening, a primitive long-distance teleconference was held with all the owners and president of the hotel. During the brainstorming session, it was suggested that the hotel be renamed the Queen City Plaza. However, due to all the furnishings having to be rebranded, someone suggested that they incorporate *Netherland Plaza* into the name. At the time the Sherry Netherland Plaza in New York was a decadent hotel in the Big Apple. If they added the last name of the developer, William A. Starrett and his brother, Paul who served as the chairman of the board, they would be able to keep the prized *St. NP* lettering all over the hotel. After hashing it out for an hour or two, the group agreed to rename the new hotel, *the Starrett Netherland Plaza*.

The Starrett Netherland Plaza was not merely one of the most lavish hotels in Ohio; it was an opulent masterpiece. From its intricate ceiling murals to the exquisite Brazilian Rosewood paneling, every detail spoke of luxury and grandeur. The hotel boasted a mesmerizing Rockwood Pottery fountain, a vibrant nightclub, a delightful array of seven restaurants, and even a charming wedding chapel. This extravagant French art deco establishment stood among the finest hotels in the entire United States.

The dedication to luxury did not stop at the hotel's lobby; it extended to each of the 800 rooms. These accommodations were equipped with modern amenities, such as running water, a cutting-edge four-station A.M. radio, and even a telephone. No expense was spared in ensuring that every guest experienced the epitome of comfort and convenience.

A year after its name change, the Starrett Hotel underwent a transition when it was acquired by John Emery Jr, a prominent local businessman. Consequently, the property went through multiple rebranding efforts over the following five decades as ownership changed hands.

Over the course of more than half a century, the Carew Tower endured the effects of weathering, including wear and tear, and the corrosive impact of salt during wintertime. Eventually, in the 1980s, the entire complex necessitated extensive renovation due to safety concerns surrounding certain beams and concrete structures. Between 1982 and 1994, a comprehensive remodeling project was undertaken to bring the  Carew Tower and the entire complex up to code, ensuring its compliance with relevant regulations and standards.

In recognition of its historical significance, the hotel received the distinction of being designated a National Historic Landmark in 1994. Presently, it is owned and operated by Hilton. Despite its nearly century-old existence, the hotel continues to be one of the most sought-after destinations in the city.

Hauntings

With almost a century of history to draw from, surely there have to be some ghost stories in the Netherland Plaza, right?

According to staff members, the hotel is haunted by a woman that is often referred to as *"The Lady in Green"*. The mysterious female phantom has been spotted in various places around the hotel. In fact, she was even photographed on the 25th floor by a guest in May 2022. I was told that a handful of hotel employees even have a copy of the photo on their phone.

While wrapping up this project, I spent the night in the Netherlands Plaza Hotel in March 2023. After asking around to various associates, I heard all about the picture of the entity, but no one seemed to have a copy. However, as I was headed downstairs to check out, I randomly ran into a security guard who knew all about the Lady in Green. In fact, when I asked him if he knew about the alleged picture, he told me that he had a picture of her on his phone and asked if I wanted to see it!

Sure enough, like other staff members had mentioned, the woman in the photo was wearing a green dress as she stood in the hallway of the 25th floor.

Naturally, I immediately took the elevator back to the 25th floor and took some pictures. Unfortunately, I was not able to capture the Lady in Green.

But who is the Lady in Green? Why has she decided to stick around the hotel? There are a plethora of unbelievable stories, but they all seem to center 'round a tragic event that occurred during the construction of the Carew Tower.

On May 26, 1930, tragedy struck when Joseph Luerck, a skilled 34-year-old electrician, was carrying out the installation of electrical equipment in a hotel elevator shaft on the sixth floor. As fate would have it, an unfortunate moment led to his loss of balance while reaching for a screwdriver. In a desperate attempt to regain stability, Luerck instinctively reached out for a nearby cable. Regrettably, the cable proved to be just beyond his grasp. The consequences were dire, as Luerck plummeted a staggering sixty feet, tragically breaking his neck upon impact in the building's basement. The arrival of Dr. J. R. Nielauder brought the somber realization that this young man's life had been tragically cut short. With a heavy heart, Dr. Nielauder officially pronounced Joseph Luerck dead at the scene.

This is where the story branches out and gets a little muddy. Some variations of the tale say that after the funeral, Luerck's wife came to the hotel to visit the sixth floor to see where her husband fell. Once she got to the spot, the young lady was so overcome by grief that she jumped headfirst into the elevator shaft.

Another variation of the story says that she waited until the night of the hotel's grand opening. After checking in, the grieving widow went to the sixth floor and shimmied the elevator doors open. She stood there for a moment reflecting on her life and how miserable she was without her beloved Joseph. Like the other version of the tale, it ends with Mrs. Luerck at the bottom of the elevator shaft with a broken neck.

While the stories are legendary, there is no evidence that a woman died from falling down the elevator shaft.

Mysteriously, the hotel staff have seen the enigmatic presence known as "the Lady in Green" inside the elevator. According to hotel legend, the peculiar

encounter occurred approximately fifteen years ago when an employee entered the elevator to deliver room service to one of the upper floors. During the ascent, the staff member engaged in pleasant conversation with a woman dressed in an elegant green gown. As soon as the elevator door opened, the staff member looked up to bid farewell, only to find the woman had mysteriously vanished!

Unusual occurrences within the confines of the elevator have become a recurring theme among the hotel employees. Indeed, these peculiar anomalies sporadically manifest themselves, adding to the mystique surrounding this intriguing space.

"One day I was in the elevators going up and the numbers started flickering," explained a longtime desk agent. "All of a sudden, the numbers started going crazy. It went 1, 2, 3 and then jumped to 100. We don't even have a hundredth floor in the hotel!

They got someone from maintenance to look at it, but weird stuff still happens in those elevators."

The Lady in Green isn't limited to the elevator, she's also been spotted in the Hall of Mirrors ballroom. Each time, she wore the beautiful green dress that she is known for.

Several years ago, a lady was leaving a banquet being held in the Hall of Mirrors when she noticed an unfamiliar lady in a green dress that seemed out of place. When the woman walked over to say hello and introduce herself, the Lady in Green disappeared right in front of her!

But it's not just apparitions that catch the attention of hotel staff and guests. The Lady in Green can be quite mischievous and messes with those that work there.

"I don't go to the 25th floor," said one unnerved desk agent. "I know that's where the Lady in Green stays. I have been up there, and the hallway will suddenly get icy cold like someone left a window open in January, but it is the middle of June!

But what really creeps me out about the 25th floor is room 2540. I've worked overnight and we will get calls at the front desk from that room! Each time I pick up, there is no one there. There is no voice or anyone breathing, it's only a strange scratching sound. I get chills just thinking about it! The first time it happened, another desk agent told me someone staying in the room knew the hotel was haunted and was playing a prank on me. I went right away and checked the computer. No one was in 2540 that night!"

The hotel not only experiences paranormal activity throughout its premises but also holds an eerie reputation for its haunted basement, where the fitness center and pool are situated. Even employees who work in this lower level have reported witnessing unexplainable phenomena while going about their duties.

"There were times I'd come in around 3:30 and the pool would be shut down and the lights were off," explained the gym manager. "There was no one there but I'd see a

shadow walking back in the pool area. It was like someone was walking around but when I'd go back there and look, no one was there. It happened more than once. I just got used to it.

The whole hotel is haunted. Everyone has stories if they've been around long enough."

Faux Phantoms

The Screamer

One fateful night in July of 1891, Meyer Helwitz, the sexton of the United Jewish Cemetery, found himself unable to find solace within the confines of his quarters on the cemetery grounds. The oppressive heat of the summer air left him restless and agitated, causing him to toss and turn for what felt like an eternity. Eventually, succumbing to his restlessness, Helwitz made the decision to rise from his bed and indulge in the companionship of a well-deserved cigar.

Weary and unable to find respite in slumber, the aging grave digger embarked on an impromptu journey, clad in his pajamas, through the solemn expanse of the burial grounds. As he meandered amidst the somber presence of gravestones, basking in the ethereal glow of the full moon above, Helwitz's senses were abruptly assaulted by a piercing, terror-stricken scream, tearing through the tranquil night. It was swiftly followed by the disconcerting cacophony of a horse-drawn carriage grinding to an abrupt halt.

With a surge of adrenaline, the elderly man sprinted with all his might towards the gates, where a peculiar sight awaited him. There, in the middle of the road, stood a carriage, its occupants enveloped in a flurry of panic. The desperate man within struggled fervently to revive his fainting wife, who lay helpless before him.

Driven by compassion, Helwitz hastened back to his humble abode, retrieving a vessel of water to aid the ailing woman. As she gradually regained consciousness, she tremulously recounted her harrowing experience.

It appeared that while passing by the cemetery, her gaze had been transfixed upon a specter dressed in billowing white, gliding eerily above the resting places of the departed. However, much to her astonishment, Helwitz burst into uproarious laughter, dispelling her fears with a simple revelation: the apparition she had witnessed was none other than the nocturnal wanderings of the old sexton himself.

Trouble on the Little Miami

In July 1883, an elderly Irish widow named Mrs. O'Rourke relocated to a house near the Little Miami Depot. However, shortly after moving in, she hastily packed her belongings and informed her neighbors that she couldn't endure living in a house infested with rowdy spirits.

Naturally, the neighbors began discussing the matter, which eventually caught the attention of a reporter from the Cincinnati Post. Intrigued, the journalist interviewed the residents of the neighborhood and conducted some research. It was then revealed that Mrs. O'Rourke's residence had a sordid past, having once been a notorious brothel and a saloon where multiple men had lost their lives many years ago.

With the pieces of the puzzle falling into place, the reporter made arrangements with the landlord to spend a night in the house, accompanied by a friend for support in case any mischievous spirits were indeed present. After settling in for the night, the duo embarked on a self-guided exploration of the building before making themselves comfortable on the first floor. As the evening wore on, the amateur ghost hunters engaged in conversation until the reporter's companion dozed off. Half an hour later, the journalist himself fell asleep.

Suddenly, the writer was jolted awake by the sound of footsteps echoing through the house. Startled, he reached for his lamp, only to hear the shuffling feet drawing nearer and nearer!

Uncertain of what action to take, the reporter abandoned the idea of illuminating the room and opted to lie perfectly still, hoping to witness the apparitions materialize. However, as he lay on the floor, he felt something damp gently brush against his nose.

Consumed by fear, the man realized that the ghost was right beside him! Disturbed by the journalist's movements, his friend awakened and anxiously inquired, "Has the ghost arrived?"

Before the startled companion could receive an answer, the reporter swiftly grabbed his revolver and lit his lantern. In the glow of the light, both men were astonished to witness half a dozen skunks scurrying away into the darkness of an adjacent room.

The Man in White

After completing his cleaning duties at Vine Street schoolhouse on the night of May 8, 1897, the janitor, Fred Hoering, was about to leave the building when something peculiar caught his attention. As he leisurely walked into the dimly lit alley behind the school, Hoering was startled to the core when he noticed an enigmatic figure dressed entirely in white, standing about twenty feet ahead. What made it even more eerie was the luminous glow emanating from the phantom's face, with its eyes and mouth appearing to illuminate.

Overwhelmed with panic, the frightened custodian immediately blew on a police whistle that he habitually carried around his neck. In a matter of minutes, half a dozen police officers hurried to the scene to aid Hoering. Despite their disbelief, the officers cautiously encircled the menacing apparition, forming a semicircle around it. Upon receiving a signal, the daring policemen mustered the courage to approach.

Surprisingly, as they lunged towards the figure, it did not vanish into thin air as one might expect!

After a brief struggle, the towering specter was wrestled to the ground, and laughter erupted among the officers. To their astonishment, there was no ghost at all. It turned out that mischievous schoolchildren had crafted a life-sized man out of paper and affixed it to a fence in the alley. To add to the eerie effect, they had placed a lantern behind the makeshift head, casting a haunting glow throughout the dark passage.

The commotion caused quite a stir on Vine Street, attracting residents who emerged from their homes to witness the spectacle. The following morning, the ghostly tale found its way into the local newspapers, forever etching this memorable incident into the annals of the community's history.

Seances & Spiritualism

Dr. Slade Comes to Cincinnati

Dr. Henry Slade emerged as one of the most contentious spiritualists in 19th-century America. His spiritual journey began in Michigan during his childhood, and he later sought advanced training from experienced mediums in New York before venturing to England in the 1870s.

Dr. Slade developed a distinctive expertise in conducting séances, claiming the ability to communicate with spirits using a slate during intimate sessions. While many spiritualists of the era relied on energy chambers, which were essentially spacious cabinets used to create mysterious sounds, Slade took a different approach with his slate-based communication.

Dr. Slade had a unique approach to his consultations, preferring to meet individuals privately and charging them $50 for his time. During these sessions, he would hold the hand of the person seeking his assistance and slide a slate and pencil under the table. It was believed that spirits would use the pencil provided to write messages on the slate.

Opinions about Dr. Slade's abilities varied. Some were convinced that he possessed a remarkable gift from the realm beyond, while others dismissed him as a charlatan. In the 1880s, during his time in Nashville, a lady approached him and paid a small fee for a session. As their time drew to a close, the woman casually mentioned the recent passing of her brother, expressing her desire to communicate with him. Although Dr. Slade couldn't establish contact with her deceased sibling, he astonishingly revealed precise details about the brother's cause of death, despite having no prior knowledge of the man or his circumstances prior to the session.

On the other hand, Dr. Slade had a bad reputation amongst other spiritualists. He had been caught writing messages on a slate with a flesh-colored thimble in New York and was also thrown in jail in London in 1876. While performing in England, he was found in possession of slates with pre-written messages. When he got out on appeal, Dr. Slade fled to America and started touring large cities like Chicago, Kansas City, Cincinnati and Louisville to make a living. It was rumored that Dr. Slade was up to his old tricks using prewritten messages on the slates, but it was never proven.

Some skeptics swore that he wrote the messages with his toes. By holding his patient's hand, Dr. Slade made it impossible for them to break away and look under the table to see if anything nefarious was going on.

However, Dr. Slade pulled it off, legitimately or not, he stayed one step ahead of everyone and bounced around from city to city while avoiding places where he had been accused of being a fraud.

In mid-January 1882, Dr. Slade arrived in Cincinnati and checked into the opulent Hotel Emery. Word quickly spread around town and a reporter from the Enquirer paid him a visit.

Dr. Slade graciously welcomed the young writer into his room, engaging in polite conversation before delving into the intricacies of his life. The enigmatic figure shared anecdotes about his upbringing in Chautauqua County, New York, and his subsequent relocation to Michigan, where he stumbled upon an extraordinary talent. Despite acknowledging his past overseas troubles, Dr. Slade assured the journalist that he had been exonerated and was able to return to the United States without impediment.

Regrettably, during his arduous journey back home, Dr. Slade fell victim to a debilitating stroke that left him paralyzed on his right side and robbed him of vision in his right eye. Upon reaching San Francisco, he sought the assistance of a renowned healer known for his primal methods and promptly scheduled an appointment. Astonishingly, within mere minutes of their encounter, Dr. Slade's right eye regained its sight, and the mobility on his right side was miraculously restored.

After hearing the medium's life story, the interview took a turn and the writer asked Dr. Slade to defend himself against accusations that he was a fraud. Instantly, the doctor's demeanor changed from friendly to defiant as he seemed to be annoyed by the question. Dr. Slade insisted that if he were able to produce the writings on the slates, then he would be a much wealthier man than he is. Sensing the aggravation in Dr. Slade's tone, the Enquirer employee thanked him for his time and left the hotel.

A few days later, the same writer visited a local medium, Professor S. S. Baldwin. Irritated that Dr. Slade had come to his hometown to poach potential clients, Professor Baldwin berated the slippery spiritualist that he accused of resorting to trickery to achieve manifestations from the other side.

According to Professor Baldwin, he had been intrigued with Dr. Slade and made an appointment to sit with him in New York in 1874. Skeptical about whether the doctor was legitimate, Professor Baldwin set up a trap that Dr. Slade eagerly fell into.

During the session with Dr. Slade, Professor Baldwin never told him what his name was and spent most of their time together talking about his deceased father (who was really still alive).

After talking about his late dad with the medium, Professor Baldwin left his hat behind. Inside the brim, he had written a fake name, Jim Hervey. Pretending like he had forgotten it; the professor went back to Dr. Slade's room to ask for it. When the doctor opened the door, he informed his client that he had just received a communication from the spirit world from someone named Hervey who had a message for Jim. Professor Baldwin played along and told the doctor that it must have been his father trying to reach him from the other side.

In his quest to unravel the secrets behind Dr. Slade's baffling feats, Professor Baldwin maintained regular visits to the enigmatic mystic over the following months. Rather than delving into personal matters concerning his late father, the professor would tirelessly recount tales of a recent bereavement, involving the loss of his beloved girlfriend. Picking up on his client's grief, Dr. Slade began summoning the restless spirit of a young lady who would appear in the dark under the table while the seances were being held. With each subsequent session, the spectral woman grew bolder, reaching out to touch Professor Baldwin's leg and calling out to him from the shadows.

One night after Dr. Slade conjured the ethereal apparition, Professor Baldwin seized the opportunity to expose the deceitful magician. Swiftly, he ignited a phosphorus-based light bomb, casting a blinding radiance upon the room. In the ensuing chaos, the professor deftly reached down, grasping the figure beneath the table, and guided them towards a nearby lamp. Bathed in the newfound illumination, the truth was unveiled — instead of a lady, it was a gangly sixteen-year-old boy!

As Dr. Slade struggled to regain his composure, he implored the professor not to expose his charade, a plea born out of desperation. To the astonishment of many, Professor Baldwin opted against revealing the deceitful magician's true nature. His sole objective had been to uncover the methods by which Dr. Slade deceived and manipulated his audiences, harboring no immediate desire to ruin him — unless came back Cincinnati.

To prove that Dr. Slade was a fraud, Professor Baldwin gave the reporter $150. He asked him to tell his old friend that he could have the money if he could produce a manifestation in his presence that the professor himself couldn't duplicate.

Realizing he was onto a big story, the eager reporter went back to Hotel Emery and knocked on the door of room 108 where Dr. Slade was staying. Dr. Slade recognized the young journalist and invited him to come into his room. The reporter informed the medium that Professor Baldwin had called him out and he wanted to give him an opportunity to respond. He even brought a blank slate for Doctor Slade in case he wanted to clear his name.

Though the ambitious journalist was ready for an impromptu séance, the spirits were not, according to Dr. Slade. Stumbling over his words, the dubious doctor explained that it was too late to have a session and that he never gave sittings between five and seven o'clock.

The writer, naturally, requested to return the next day. Dr. Slade gestured towards a table with a stack of cards, revealing that he had over fifty people waiting for a session. Despite his packed schedule, Dr. Slade reluctantly consented to the reporter's visit at 4 o'clock the following afternoon. His only condition was that the he came alone.

During that time Professor Baldwin amended his offer to Dr. Slade. Instead of $50 per manifestation, he would pay $50 per word that the doctor could get the spirits to write in front of him. So, when the reporter showed up at his hotel on Sunday, January 25th at the designated time, he immediately relayed this information to the medium when he answered the door. However, the writer quickly realized that Dr. Slade wasn't the only person in the room.

When Dr. Slade opened the door, the journalist saw F. B. Plimpton, the editor of the Cincinnati Commercial smoking a cigar. Realizing that the doctor was about to hold a séance, Plimpton asked if he could finish his cigar and watch the session.

Initially, Dr. Slade agreed to his friend's request but when Plimpton casually mentioned that he didn't believe that manifestations were supernatural, Dr. Slade backpedaled. Since he had insisted that the writer come alone, Dr. Slade thought it wouldn't be fair for someone to sit in and observe the séance. Yet, the doctor would allow the newspaper editor to join in as long as he agreed to come sit with the pair at the table. Plimpton agreed and Dr. Slade began seating his guests.

Dr. Slade sat across from Plimpton and the young writer was placed at the end of the table between them. Even though Dr. Slade agreed to use a slate provided by the writer, he grabbed one off a table and cleaned it. Before placing the handpicked slate on the floor, he presented it to both men for inspection.

With the slate under the table, Dr. Slade insisted that both men join hands with him near the center of the table. After a few moments, a slight tapping was heard, and the mystic picked up the tablet and showed it to the writer. As he placed it next to his ear, the Enquirer reporter could hear what sounded like Dr. Slade tapping on the slate with his finger.

When the tapping stopped, Dr. Slade pulled the slate from the journalist's ear and showed both he and Mr. Plimpton. On the slate was a short message about spiritualism by an unknown spirit named *C. Martin*.

During the session, the reporter also felt something grabbing his legs and witnessed a slate rise up from the floor and place itself on the table. Having been warned by Professor Baldwin about Dr. Slade's incredible strength in his toes and feet, the journalist dismissed what he saw as a campy parlor trick. But there was more chicanery. After Dr. Slade requested that both men move closer to the table, he felt something jerk his chair and saw the table rise several inches. While Plimpton was blown away, the journalist noticed that the doctor's body shifted, and he appeared to be moving things again with his legs and feet.

Dr. Slade astutely observed ethereal figures lingering around the reporter, intriguing him to inscribe the name of a departed individual on the blank slate and position it face down upon the table. Drawing inspiration from Professor Baldwin's prior demonstration, the journalist hastily penned the name of his still-living mother. Subsequently, Dr. Slade discreetly concealed it beneath the table, only to retrieve it shortly thereafter. Stealing a furtive glance at the inscription, Dr. Slade inquired if the person identified on the slate was of the female gender. The reporter silently nodded, affirming the medium's intuitive perception. Delving deeper into the matter, the clairvoyant dared to ascertain if the individual in question was indeed the journalist's mother. Once again, the young man nodded, and an exhilarated Plimpton could hardly contain his enthusiasm at witnessing Dr. Slade's remarkable ability to connect with spirits.

When the slate was flipped over it revealed a message from the reporter's mother (who was still alive)

Oh, My Dear Son: I hope you will not doubt this, for it is true. We do live and can return after what is called death. I am often by you to impress you to do right. Believe me to be your loving mother.

As Dr. Slade ended the session, an excited F. B. Plimpton thanked both men for allowing him to attend the séance and politely excused himself. When the two were finally alone, the journalist placed a blank slate on the table and asked Dr. Slade if the spirits could write something on it when it wasn't under the table and obstructed from view. The doctor insisted that it could be done but sadly, all the spirits had left for the evening. Not backing down, the writer asked if he could come back another day when the spirits were more active. Yet, Dr. Slade maintained that his schedule was booked and didn't think he could fit him in any time soon.

The following day, The Enquirer published a scathing article penned by a writer who accused Dr. Slade of employing deceptive tactics akin to cheap parlor tricks, all aimed at fabricating an illusion of spiritual presence within the room. The writer firmly believed that the doctor cunningly concealed prewritten slates amidst the foliage of the table, deftly swapping them with a sleight of hand before presenting them to his unsuspecting guests.

Unsurprisingly, Dr. Slade's departure from Cincinnati didn't delay itself. Mere days following the article's publication, the fraudulent clairvoyant swiftly gathered his belongings and embarked on a journey southward to Louisville.

Professor Johnson & Little Susie

After making a splash summoning the spirits of notable people like President George Washington, Professor D. S. Johnson scheduled an event on May 17, 1892, at a small venue on Oliver Street. To promote the demonstration, Professor Johnson told people that he would summon the spirits of two recently deceased prominent citizens, John Woodruff and John Nordlah. Unbeknownst to him, on the night of the show the skeptical widows of Woodruff and the sister of Nordlah paid fifty cents to attend the event.

During the captivating demonstration, Professor Johnson confidently strode into his cabinet, assuring the audience that the spirit of John Woodruff, the esteemed former editor of the Cincinnati Times, was about to make a remarkable appearance. As anticipation filled the air, a luminous figure emerged from the shadows, gracefully approaching the mesmerized guests. With an air of intrigue, Professor Johnson presented his ethereal guest, extending an invitation for anyone in the audience to share their thoughts or wishes with the otherworldly presence.

Woodruff's widow, positioned in the front row, voiced her desire to communicate with her late husband. The spectral figure, donning a white shroud, cautiously approached the woman as she proceeded to inquire about their relationship and family. Regrettably, his responses fell short of satisfying her curiosity. The apparition then reached out to Mrs. Woodruff, grasping her hand before leaning in for a kiss. This act of intimacy provoked an intense rage within the widow, prompting her to forcefully strike the phantom. A commotion ensued as individuals rushed in to intervene and separate the conflicting pair. Meanwhile, Professor Johnson burst out of his cabinet, livid, and demanded the immediate expulsion of Mrs. Woodruff. Despite the professor's outburst, the determined widow adamantly maintained her position, asserting her right to remain for the entire demonstration since she had paid fifty cents. With muttered profanities under his breath, Professor Johnson begrudgingly returned to his cabinet, preparing to recommence the session.

Once order was restored, Professor Johnson made a captivating announcement - the spirit of John Nordlah had supposedly joined their gathering. However, the excitement quickly turned into skepticism as Nordlah's sister vehemently expressed her disbelief, asserting that the white figure before her bore no resemblance to her beloved brother. Sensing the tension, the spirit retreated to the safety of the cabinet, and the room was illuminated once again as the lamps flickered back to life, signaling the conclusion of the evening.

Professor Johnson was slammed in the local papers and called a fraud by both ladies at the show. After the hubbub, the medium laid low for a while to let things blow over.

But Professor Johnson wasn't done with the controversial cabinet sessions.

A year later, Professor Johnson was back holding demonstrations in his home on West Eighth Street. On Thursday night, July 27th, 1893, twenty people packed into his parlor to witness what promised to be an eventful night. Yet, Unbeknown to the professor, half of those in attendance were members of the Ohio Liberal Society, a group of like-minded individuals who weren't fans of phony spiritualists.

Professor D. S. Johnson

Before commencing the demonstration, Professor Johnson extended a warm invitation to everyone, urging them to inspect his cabinet before settling into their seats. He kindly requested that each individual maintain an upright posture, observe absolute silence, and avoid any unnecessary movement. Crossing one's legs, he emphasized, was discouraged as it was believed to create an unwelcoming atmosphere for spirits. Once the group was arranged in a semicircle, facing the mysterious cabinet in the dimly lit room, the professor initiated the session by leading a recitation of the Lord's Prayer. As he led the group in a hymn, Professor Johnson explained that music was necessary to produce spirits and then played sounds from a music box.

Professor Johnson's cabinet

In the parlor, a large tin trumpet tumbled out of the cabinet, resonating with a faint melody. It was followed by the soft voice of a woman. Among the gathered crowd, a lady in the back exclaimed that the voice belonged to her beloved mother, who had departed from this world years ago. Professor Johnson graciously invited her to pose any questions she wished. With a touch of nervousness in her voice, the lady called out, "Mother, is that really you?"

A clear "Yes" resonated through the room, confirming her suspicions.

Emboldened by the response, the lady continued, directing her inquiry to her departed mother, "Are you happy?"

The matronly voice reassured her, "I am."

At that moment, Professor Johnson made the exciting proclamation that the first spirit was about to materialize. A peculiar rustling filled the room, adding an air of anticipation, while the professor proceeded to chant a hymn. Unexpectedly, a radiant glow emanated from the cabinet, unveiling the presence of a man adorned with a lengthy, ebony beard, garbed entirely in white.

A woman, overwhelmed with emotion, exclaimed, "That's my husband!" Professor Johnson encouraged her to approach, urging her to observe closely if the spirit would provide a sign. With great urgency, the lady called out, "Husband, raise your right hand!" As if responding to her plea, the apparition slowly elevated his right hand, only to vanish into thin air, leaving an aura of wonder and awe in its wake.

Moments later, a captivating scene unfolded as a baby girl, named Little Susie, materialized in the room. However, to the surprise of the perplexed audience, her identity remained a mystery. The spectators, seemingly disinterested in the child, watched as she gradually faded away, leaving behind an air of intrigue. Suddenly, emerging from the very same cabinet, a diminutive figure with a distinguished beard made his entrance.

Without any forewarning or formal introduction, the bearded phantom found himself being abruptly tackled by John F. Lawrence, a member of the Ohio Liberal Society. Chaos erupted as women shrieked in alarm, but the resilient apparition managed to gain the upper hand, pinning Lawrence down. Sensing the urgency of the situation, two fellow associates from the anti-spiritualist group leaped into action, wielding small, illuminated pocket lamps. Acting swiftly, they intervened, successfully prying the two combatants apart.

In a moment of revelation, as Lawrence clutched onto the phantom's face, a cunning disguise was revealed—a fake beard! Standing there, holding the deceptive facial hair, the protester exclaimed, "It's a woman!"

As all hell was breaking loose around him, Professor Johnson swiftly retrieved a club concealed within a secret compartment of the cabinet. In a desperate attempt to defend himself, he swung the weapon at Lawrence. Regrettably, much like the bearded woman, his efforts proved futile as he was promptly overpowered and wrestled to the ground.

Surrounded by a group of ten members from the Ohio Liberal Society, Professor Johnson begged for mercy and implored the men not to kill him.

Due to the ruckus going on inside the house, three police officers on patrol broke Professor Johnson's door down and barged in. Believing a fire had broken out, firefighters also raced to the scene with ladders in hand. With three hundred curiosity seekers standing in the street watching, several members of the Ohio Liberal Society explained to the authorities what had happened and agreed to testify against Professor Johnson.

When police arrested the bearded phantom, she was identified as a 35-year-old female, Ida Juliet. Juliet was allowed to change before she was hauled away with the professor in a patrol wagon to the Hammond Street Police Station. Officers also took a stuffed dress with a mask wrapped around it that had been presented as Little Susie earlier in the evening. When Susie was brought to the station a tag was placed on it that read, "This spirit was seized at Professor Johnson's, 25 West Eighth Street."

Under interrogation, Professor Johnson admitted he was a 40-year-old harness maker who also worked as a "trumpet medium". After attending several seances in the area he felt that was called to produce spirits as well. Together with his friend Professor Aaron Willis, the pair routinely held demonstrations and seances in Professor Johnson's home on Eight Street at 2 and 8 p.m. each day. Roughly thirty to forty people a day happily paid fifty cents to communicate with spirits that both mystics could summon.

When detectives raided Professor Johnson's home, they found a fake baby, a dressmaker, wigs, fake beards, slates and books coated with phosphorus. Inside the books were pages containing generic names of people that the medium could summon during a demonstration.

A spiritualist who had participated in numerous seances at the professor's residence arrived at the station, demanding to press charges. This devout follower claimed to have given Professor Johnson a substantial amount of money and insisted on legal action against him.

After an extensive investigation, Professor Johnson and Ida Juliet were charged with practicing a trick game and obtaining money under false pretenses. However, the charges were subsequently dropped and replaced with a violation of the Russell law, which mandated that practicing spiritualists pay and annual fee of $1,000 to the city.

While in custody, Professor Johnson engaged in a conversation with a reporter from his jail cell, vehemently asserting his forthcoming vindication. According to him, there was a small group of people that hated mediums who were determined to ruin his good name. The slippery spiritualist told the reporter that his second, Ida Juliet, had been asking for a larger percentage of the money collected and that she was doing things in the demonstrations that he didn't approve of. The professor firmly believed that Ida intentionally conducted herself in a suspicious manner during the seances, with the ulterior motive of casting him in a negative light.

In lieu of a trial, Professor Johnson requested to perform a demonstration for the prosecutor and judge. Ultimately, he was denied.

After Professor D. S. Johnson's unfortunate exposure, his close friend and partner, Professor Aaron Willis, endeavored to defend him in the media, albeit acknowledging the regrettable nature of the situation. During an interview with a local reporter, he candidly stated, "When I get to the point that trickery becomes necessary, I will retire from the business."

Despite the circumstances, Professor Willis remained steadfast in his belief in the legitimacy of Professor Johnson's abilities, emphasizing his esteemed position within the spiritualist community. He highlighted that the revelations brought forth during Professor Johnson's seances surpassed the limits of human knowledge. However, he acknowledged the notion that mediums could potentially lose their powers due to indulgence in alcohol or a morally compromised lifestyle. He speculated that his colleague might be grappling with personal issues that could be affecting his abilities.

After Professor Johnson tarnished the reputation of spiritualism, Professor Willis was determined to establish his own credibility. Seeking to prove his legitimacy, he reached out to a reporter from the Cincinnati Post and extended an invitation to witness a private demonstration at his residence. Eagerly accepting the offer, the writer arrived on the evening of August 1st, 1893.

Professor Aaron Willis

When the journalist arrived, Professor Willis welcomed him into his parlor where a few other guests were already seated. The gathering began with a recitation of the Lord's Prayer. Suddenly, there was a loud knock, and Professor Willis approached the center of the room. After greeting his guests, he moved to a corner as the lights dimmed. A trumpet floated in the air and landed near the representative from the Cincinnati Post. A commanding voice, that of a spirit named John Morris, exclaimed, "I'm very glad to see you! The spirits have just had word of the proposed test seances desired by the Post and have taken the project under careful consideration. We want to do everything possible for the newspapers when we believe it to be in the interest of spiritualism and the Post's general fairness in matters leads us to look with favor upon the test seances. Personally, I am glad to see you and to recognize the fact that there is a gentleman at the larger end of the trumpet."

One by one, a series of ethereal white figures emerged from the cabinet and approached the reporter, gently patting him on the head.

Over the next thirty minutes, various spirits entered and exited the cabinet, warmly greeting the guests in the room. To ensure transparency and dispel any doubts of trickery, Professor Willis extended an invitation to the reporter to thoroughly examine the cabinet and explore his home.

While there were no mishaps or anything over the top at the demonstration, Professor Willis was asked to perform a session in front of an impartial jury selected by the Cincinnati Post. The confident clairvoyant agreed to hold a demonstration and the paper selected the Grand Hotel, a neutral location for August 31st.

Amidst the unfolding media frenzy, a police officer was dispatched to Professor Willis' residence with the purpose of verifying his license to practice spiritualism. Upon the officer's arrival, the professor calmly apprised him of a recent amendment to the law. While clairvoyants, astrologers, fortune tellers, and seers were obliged to obtain a license, mediums were exempted from this requirement.

Upon scrutinizing the legislation, the district attorney confirmed the accuracy of Professor Willis' assertion. Consequently, law enforcement ceased their inquiries and the charge against Professor Johnson for violating the Russell law was dropped. Still facing other charges, Professor Johnson managed to secure bail by persuading a prosperous spiritualist to provide the necessary funds. However, within a few days of regaining his freedom, the cunning clairvoyant skipped town, leaving Ida Juliet incarcerated and alone.

The Grand Hotel in Cincinnati was abuzz with anticipation on the day of Professor Willis' highly anticipated demonstration. Rumors had been circulating throughout the town about a daring incident during a previous session, where a man purportedly burst into the professor's cabinet only to be jolted to the floor by a powerful electric shock when a spirit materialized before his eyes.

Despite these astonishing accounts, some skeptics persisted in their belief that the professor's own son was masquerading as the controlling spirit named John Morris during these demonstrations. Nevertheless, no one dared to venture into the cabinet to put this theory to the test. It was rumored that Professor Willis had taken precautions, equipping the structure with a knife and a gun following an ambush on Professor Johnson by the Ohio Liberal Society.

Despite receiving numerous cards and letters with monetary offers from individuals in Kentucky, Indiana, and Ohio, expressing their interest in attending Professor Willis' demonstration, the newspaper opted to assemble a jury consisting of twelve reputable businessmen to determine the authenticity of his claims. However, Professor Willis objected to this arrangement and insisted on including spiritualists among the attendees to create more favorable conditions for manifestations. Initially, it was agreed that a small number of selected spiritualists would be permitted to participate. However, as the night of the show approached, the count of spiritualists ballooned to thirty-three.

The Ohio Liberal Society also sought permission for some of its members to be present at the event. Nonetheless, the Post declined their request, aiming to provide Professor Willis with an impartial opportunity to prove his legitimacy.

On the evening of the highly anticipated event, the bustling Grand Hotel lobby and parlors were teeming with hundreds of eager individuals, all longing for a mere glimpse of the renowned Professor Willis. In an effort to maintain order and exclusivity, diligent police officers meticulously cleared the premises, permitting entry only to those fortunate enough to grace the coveted guest list. These privileged few were granted access to the double parlor, where the mesmerizing demonstration was poised to unfold.

Precisely at 8 o'clock, the forty-five esteemed invitees were gracefully escorted to their designated seats. To prevent any unwanted commotion or exchange of skepticism amongst nonbelievers, Professor Willis astutely positioned spiritualists on both sides of the guests, ensuring an uninterrupted séance experience. With the meticulous arrangement complete, Miss Williams, the esteemed mystic's trusted second, deftly obscured the blinds and transoms with a veil of paper, instantly shrouding the room in an impenetrable cloak of darkness.

Before the demonstration started, Professor Willis addressed the rumors of the Ohio Liberal Society possibly disrupting the show and let it be known that there were two policemen in the hallway. The jumpy medium told his audience, "In case there is any disturbance, somebody is going to get badly hurt! I would almost as soon lose my life as to have any outrage successful."

Before commencing, the visibly nervous professor acknowledged the sweltering heat in the room. He expressed his concern that the humidity might impede the successful materialization of spirits yet vowed to give his best effort regardless. Having hedged his bets, Professor Willis politely requested everyone to join hands and recite the Lord's Prayer. Following the prayer, Miss Williams gracefully played "Nearer My God to Thee" on an organ nestled in the corner of the room. As the melodious tune concluded, Professor Willis confidently declared the presence of several spirits among the group. Suddenly, gasps and screams erupted from random members of the audience as ethereal hands seemingly materialized and reached out to touch them.

Amidst the ensuing chaos, John Morris briefly materialized, only to vanish moments later. The professor desperately called out to his controlling spirit, but after a brief pause, he expressed his apologies and informed the group that the humidity had made the conditions unfavorable for manifestations.

As Professor Willis attempted to summon other spirits, a German voice was heard near the organ. While everyone was turning around to see who was talking, a Native American spirit named Bright Star appeared in the center of the room. Before the indigenous entity could fade away, non-believing jurors started asking where she came from. Hesitantly, the female phantom replied that she was from Minnesota. When pressed on which tribe she belonged to, the spirit claimed that she was a Choctaw. One of the individuals in the group, a longtime teacher, promptly corrected her, pointing out that the Choctaw Indians were not originally from Minnesota but rather from Mississippi and Alabama. Instead of offering a defense, Bright Star swiftly vanished.

After the grilling by members of the jury, the spirit of John Morris suddenly reappeared and wound down the proceedings by asking the group to sing a hymn. A moment or so later, a frazzled Professor Willis came to the center of the room and asked everyone to recite the Lord's Prayer. Immediately, someone spoke up and asked if it was possible for another spirit to materialize even though John Morris had retired for the evening.

Professor Willis stuttered and stammered before shouting, "The conditions are not favorable!" At that moment the lights were turned back on and everyone in attendance was allowed to inspect the cabinet.

Members of the Cincinnati Post summoned the jury members into the back parlor and asked them if they believed that Professor Willis was indeed an authentic medium. It was a unanimous vote. Professor Aaron Willis was a fraud.

M. A. McRae, who had been selected as chairman of the jury summed it up best, "It was a decided failure," said McRae. "There were no spirits present."

The prevailing belief was that the professor's assistant, Miss Williams, portrayed the character of Bright Star, a young squaw with an unknown origin. It was also noted that on several occasions during the evening, she played the organ prior to a spirit materializing. The jury speculated that this was done to mask the sounds of the medium or his associates changing clothes and moving around.

Following the publication of the jury's findings by the Post, Professor Willis remained defiant and vehemently denied being a fraud. He argued that the Post had not acted in good faith, failing to disclose the identities of the jurors. The medium also claimed to have conversed with jury members after the demonstration, suggesting that the newspaper had either misrepresented their statements or neglected to interview them at all.

A newsletter focused on spiritualism came forward to defend Willis, asserting that the conditions in the room were not conducive to properly see a spirit. The publication also contended that the jury members present lacked familiarity with spiritualistic phenomena and failed to comprehend what they were witnessing.

In the aftermath of the debacle and the negative press, Professor Willis adopted a lower profile. However, over the following year, he began refining his performance and placed greater emphasis on slate writing.

Professor D. S. Johnson was tracked down in Kansas City and extradited back to Cincinnati. However, despite his return, the District Attorney deemed the evidence insufficient to secure a conviction, leading to his release. Undeterred, Professor Johnson promptly returned to Missouri, where he resumed his cabinet demonstrations in the area.

As for his old partner, Ida Juliet, she was eventually released from jail and had all the charges dropped.

But that's not the end of the story.

After Professor Johnson skipped town, Joseph Wilms, a member of the Ohio Liberal Society, who helped bring him down, procured Little Susie from the district attorney. Wilms proudly displayed the "spirit" in his jewelry store on Vine Street.

One day, Al, the 22-year-old son of Professor Johnson, unexpectedly entered the shop. Unaware of Al's identity, Wilms engaged in casual conversation with him. After exchanging pleasantries, Al expressed his interest in seeing Little Susie, the doll displayed in the shop. Wilms chuckled and proceeded to share the story of how he acquired the doll, walking towards the counter.

As Wilms presented the doll to Al, to everyone's surprise, Al swiftly snatched it and hurriedly fled through the door. However, his escape was short-lived as a vigilant police officer on patrol intercepted him, promptly apprehending and arresting him. Al Johnson was swiftly transported to the police station and charged with disorderly conduct. Following the payment of a fine, he was subsequently released.

Little Susie was safely returned to Joseph Wilms, who proudly displayed the doll in a dedicated showcase within his jewelry store for several years.

The End of the World

After serving as a captain in the 30th Infantry of the United States Army during the War of 1812, William Miller returned to his hometown of Low Hampton, New York, intending to live a quiet life as a farmer. However, deeply affected by the atrocities he had witnessed in the war and grieving the recent loss of his father and sister, Miller sought solace in the pages of the Bible. His growing faith led him to become increasingly involved in a local Baptist church, eventually leading him to start preaching in 1818.

Miller's sermons predominantly revolved around the second coming of Christ and the notion of the End of Days. Yet, his preaching went beyond mere words. He firmly believed that these events were imminent. In his extensive scriptural research, two verses stood out to this self-taught minister.

Daniel 8: 14
And he said unto me, unto two thousand and three hundred days; then shall the sanctuary be cleansed.

Ezekiel 4:6
And when thou hast accomplished them, lie again on thy right side, and thou shalt bear the iniquity of the house of Judah forty days: I have appointed thee each day for a year.

As he tried to pin down the day that his Lord and Savior would return, Miller interpreted the sanctuary being cleansed as a metaphor for when the earth would be destroyed. By applying the day per year unit of measurement from Ezekiel, he devised a complex numerological formula based on the reign of Artaxerxes that began in 457 B. C. After crunching all the numbers and dates, William Miller was certain that mankind would end sometime between March 21st, 1843, and March 21st, 1844.

William Miller

Miller preached all over the east coast and urged everyone to be prepared for when the Lord returned. Without social media and the internet, the doomsday prophet printed pamphlets and publications with his message and charts that foretold the end of humanity.

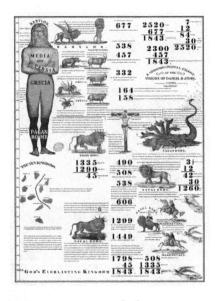

After sixteen of Miller's articles were published in the Vermont Telegram in 1832, his message went viral, and he was invited all over the country to speak. One place that Miller's message resonated the most was Cincinnati, Ohio.

During that period, Cincinnati stood as one of America's largest cities, attracting a significant number of individuals who embraced the teachings of the Millerite movement. Embracing their leader's message with utmost seriousness, these dedicated followers adopted a lifestyle that reflected the imminent end of the world.

Initially, the Millerites gathered for worship at Cincinnati College located on Fourth and Walnut Streets. However, their controversial presence there eventually led to their expulsion. Undeterred, the group swiftly erected a sizable tabernacle at the intersection of Seventh and John Streets, establishing it as their new meeting place.

The End?

Miller's proclaimed deadline of March 21st, 1844, passed without the anticipated cataclysm, but surprisingly, a significant number of his followers remained steadfast in their belief. Acknowledging his error, the conscientious preacher meticulously reviewed his calculations and discovered his mistake. He came to the realization that the anticipated momentous event, the Second Coming of the Lord, would instead transpire seven months later, precisely on October 22nd, 1844.

On that morning in October, William Miller led thousands of followers up a New York mountain, gathering to pray and eagerly await the arrival of the Lord. Meanwhile, in Cincinnati, 760 miles away, a similar scene was unfolding.

In the weeks leading up to October 22nd, the Millerites had become a divisive group in the Queen City. As William Miller's deadline came and went, many in Cincinnati, as well as across the United States, grew increasingly frustrated with those who still clung to his prophecy. Families were torn apart, and businesses suffered as a result of the zealous actions of his followers. The Millerites had become so polarizing that the mayor and police were frequently called upon to intervene when conflicts erupted between believers and nonbelievers at their tabernacle.

Days before October 22nd, the Cincinnati Millerites, including blacksmiths, tanners, carpenters, and other laborers, abruptly abandoned their jobs, choosing to spend their remaining time on Earth in prayer. In fact, most of Miller's devoted followers sold or gave away all their possessions. Even a loyal believer who earned a living as a steamboat captain relinquished ownership of his boat in the days leading up to what he believed would be his last day on Earth.

According to legend, one uncertain follower, still wavering in her beliefs, sent her sons to school but included a note with them that read, "If the world ends, please send the children home."

On the morning of the awaited return of the Lord, thousands of people congregated downtown at the tabernacle to pray. The group divided, with half setting out for Brighton Hill while the others remained behind.

Dressed in white muslin robes, roughly two thousand Millerites ascended the hill to what is now Fairview Park so they could have a great view of downtown Cincinnati being decimated by fire and brimstone. The group prayed and waited, and waited, and then waited some more. No trumpets blew, nor did a giant chariot of fire carrying the Savior burst out of the clouds.

When the sun finally came up the next morning, the crowd went home to get some sleep. Nevertheless, when they woke, the Millerites reassembled on top of the hill just in case. As they started to realize that they were not going to float to heaven while Cincinnati was destroyed by a ball of fire, the group slowly dispersed and went to see if they could get their things back.

Subsequently, William Miller, facing the consequences of his miscalculation, humbly assumed responsibility for the profound misjudgment. In a candid statement, he acknowledged his error and expressed his personal disappointment. "I confess my error and acknowledge my disappointment, "said Miller. "Yet I still believe that the day of the Lord is near, even at the door!

As Miller lost all credibility and just about all of his followers, two of his members broke off and started movements of their own, the Advent Christian Church and the Seventh Day Adventists.

Printed in the USA
CPSIA information can be obtained
at www.ICGtesting.com
LVHW022120131023
760975LV00019B/157